EVERYDAY
ACTS OF
RESURGENCE

PEOPLE, PLACES, PRACTICES

DAYKEEPER PRESS is the Center for World Indigenous Studies imprint for Humanities and Social Sciences publi-cations generated by authors resulting from research, education and public policy analysis. DayKeeper publishes the Fourth World Journal bi-annually, full length books in the fields of traditional healing arts and sciences and Fourth World studies, Occasional Papers such as Good Government Research Group reports, and digital and other on-line publications. Indexing Agents include EBSCO (Ipswich, Massachusetts USA, RMIT (formerly the Royal Melbourne Institute of Technology) Melbourne, Victoria, Australia, and Gale Group, Inc. (Detroit, Michigan, USA).

Daykeeper Press
PMB 214 1001 Cooper Point Rd SW #140
Olympia, Washington 98502
USA
Tel: 1-360-450-5645
Fax: 1-360-252-6315
chair@cwis.org

ISBN-13:978-1893710269
ISBN-10:1893710262

Book Design and Production by John Ahni Schertow, Intercontinental Cry, https://intercontinentalcry.org
Front Cover Illustration by Lianne Charlie
Back Cover Photo by No'eau Peralto

Edited by Jeff Corntassel, Taiaiake Alfred, Noelani Goodyear–Ka'ōpua, Noenoe K. Silva, Hokulani Aikau, Devi Mucina

University of Victoria
Indigenous Governance
3800 Finnerty Road
Victoria BC V8P 5C2
Canada
Tel: 1-250-721-6438
Fax: 1-250-472-4724
igov@uvic.ca

University of Hawai'i
Indigenous Politics Program
Department of Political Science
2424 Maile Way
Saunders Hall, Room 640
Honolulu, Hawaii 96822 USA
Tel: 1-956-8357
Fax: 1-956-6877
indpols@hawaii.edu

Proceeds from the sale of this book go to Intercontinental Cry

Printed by CreateSpace, An Amazon.com Company

About
The Front Cover

I drew this piece in 2015 a few weeks before the arrival of a cohort of Indigenous Governance (IGOV) students and faculty from the University of Victoria (UVic) to Hawai'i. This was the fourth exchange between IGOV and students and faculty in the Indigenous Politics program at the University of Hawai'i (UHIP). At the time, I was a second year PhD student in the UHIP program and also an alum of UVic and a friend of many of the students in IGOV that year.

It was my intention to create a piece that captured the connection not only between the people in the two programs, but the two places where the exchanges happen: Vancouver Island (the ancestral homelands of the Coast Salish, Nuu-chah-nulth, and Kwakwaka'wakw Peoples) and the Hawaiian archipelago (the ancestral homelands of Kanaka 'Ōiwi). The islands are depicted at the top and bottom of the image. Spanning across it and physically linking the landmasses are migratory birds that make the trip between the West Coast and Hawai'i annually. When I shared this image with my classmates, one mentioned that she thought the birds also looked like whale flukes, which was fitting as these relations are also making the trip across the Pacific between the islands. Emerging from the left side of the image is a series of pathways, waterways, arteries: all appropriate metaphors to capture the movement and interconnectedness of resurgence practices. And finally, encompassing it all is a chain of circles intended to depict continuity. Our ancestors and our sky and water relatives have been intentionally journeying throughout the Pacific since the beginning of time. The IGOV/UHIP exchange is but a continuation of this.

My classmate, No'eau Peralto, coined the phrase "convergence of resurgence" for the IGOV/UHIP exchange that year, and it became the title of this piece.

—Lianne Charlie

About
The Back Cover

Eia Hawai'i	Here is Hawai'i
He moku, he kanaka	An island, a human
'O Wākea ke kāne	Wākea is the male
'O Papa 'o Walinu'u ka wahine	Papa, Walinu'u is the female
Hānau Ho'ohōkū, he wahine	Born was Ho'ohōkū, a female
Hānau Hāloanakalaukapalili	Born was Hāloanakalaukapalili
He keiki 'alu'alu i kanu 'ia	A still-born who was buried
A ulu a'ela he kino kalo	And grew forth the kalo
'O Hawai'i nō ke kulāiwi	Hawai'i is the ancestral homeland
Noho hou 'o Wākea iā Ho'ohōkū	Wākea united again with Ho'ohōkū
A hānau 'o Hāloa, he ali'i	And born was Hāloa, a chief
He Kanaka 'Ōiwi e	A Kanaka 'Ōiwi

Ma o nā mo'okū'auhau o ko mākou po'e kūpuna, 'ike kākou i ka pilina 'ohana ma waena o nā akua, ka 'āina, a me nā kānaka. Ua hānau 'ia mākou, ka lāhui Kanaka Hawai'i, mai ka piko like i hānau 'ia ai ke kini akua a me ka 'āina. He mau pulapula mākou na Wākea lāua 'o Papa, na lāua ka lani ākea pa'a i luna a me ka honua pa'a i lalo. A he mau maka nō ho'i mākou na Hāloa, a i 'ai ola kona kino kalo no mākou. Wahi a kahiko, he lani ko luna, he honua ko lalo. Pili nō ho'i ko ka lani me ko ka honua, ko a uka me ko a kai, ko ka 'āina a me ko ke kanaka. 'O ka piko o ko kākou ola, 'o ia nō ka piko o ke ea o ka 'āina.

Through the genealogies of our ancestors, we know the familial relationships that connect the akua, the 'āina, and the people. We, the native people of Hawai'i, were born of the same piko from which the multitude of our akua (gods) and 'āina too were born. We are the descendants of Wākea and Papa, our ancestor-

gods who are embodied in the heavenly expanse above and the earth firmly established below. We are also the offspring of Hāloa, and his body form as the kalo
is the staple that nourishes us. According to the traditions of old, "he lani ko luna,
he honua ko lalo." That of the heavens is connected to that of the earth. That of
the uplands is connected to that of the sea. And that of the ʻāina is connected to
that of the people. The piko from which our lives emerge is the very piko from
which the life and sovereignty of this ʻāina emerges.

—Noʻeau Peralto

Table of Contents

PEOPLE

PLACES

PRACTICES

BIOGRAPHIES

ndíthäk | i hear you

LIANNE CHARLIE

Tightness in my chest	Softness in my bones
Heart racing for no reason	Heart beating for a reason
Inherently scared	Inherently dän-dhá k'é
Naturally nervous	Naturally nétsät
Old memories coming back	Old memories coming back
Reminders of not being good enough	Reminders of our intentions for you
Proof that I really don't know	Proof that you really do know
Can you name the winds?	Do you hear the winds calling your name?
Relations look familiar	It is all so familiar
Same chin	Same everything
But, what's your name again?	Our name for that is chúní
Where are you from?	She'll show you where you're from
What are you doing here?	She'll show you what you're doing here

Empty vessel	Cupped hands
Taking	Making
Mistaking	Remaking
Shoulders hunched	Shoulders hunched
Gaze down	Gaze down
What a shame	What a gift
Can you speak your language?	Ndíthäk
My tongue can't make that sound	Ìhtsųma, you sound familiar
Muscle memory	Ancestral voices
Silenced	Strong
Tied	Tuned
Bound by fear	Ricocheting off mountains
You're not doing that right	Can you show me how to do this?
If you grew up here, you would know	I didn't grow up here
If you didn't leave, you would know	I had to leave
If you talked like us, you would know	I talk like this now
If you dressed different, you would know	I wear these clothes
If you walked slower, you would know	We are all walking with purpose, you know
Listen more	Níkhti more
Maybe that will help	That will help, she says
Read less	Huzhe less
Maybe that will help	That will help, she says
Tightness in my chest	Softness in my bones
Heart racing	Heart beating for a reason
Muscle memories	Ancestral voices
Pumping through my body	Drumming through my body
Pulsing	Beating
Seizing	Breathing
Remaining	Returning
Releasing	Releasing

Artist's Statement

ndíthäk | i hear you

LIANNE CHARLIE

dän-dhá k'é | northern tutchone

nétsät | strong

chúní | medicine

Ìhtsұma | great-grandmother

níkhti | dream

huzhe | shame

W HEN I THINK ABOUT MY IDENTITY as a Northern Tutchone woman who has grown up away from her homelands and largely within a mainstream, urban setting, collage helps me reconcile the seemingly irreconcilable. Collage creates a space where home/away, insider/outsider, new/old, native/non-native, city/bush can exist in productive juxtaposition. In reality, I struggle with these dichotomies. They are riddled with judgement, pain, loss and disconnection. We left the Yukon—the home of my ancestors—when I was six years old. Although I have visited numerous times since, when I move there in a year, it will be the first time in my adult life that I will live there. While I am very excited about returning to the Yukon, I realize that it will not come without its challenges. Blood-ties and memories will fuel the initial reconnection with my relatives and the broader community; but there will be a lot to learn about life in the North and a lot of people, places and things to be reacquainted with. It is precisely because of these challenges that I find the lessons embedded in collage so helpful. Collage invites us to work with the fragmented realities of Indigenous identities, families, communities, cultures, and lands that have been created (sometimes violently, often intentionally) by historical and contemporary colonialism. It brings seemingly unrelated and diverse pieces—people, places, texts, contexts, experiences, practices, histories, traditions, ontologies— into purposeful and productive juxtaposition (Allen 2012); essentially allowing for multiple and sometimes incommensurable elements to be placed within new proximities to one another (Tuck and Yang 2012). When our communities or our lives are looked at as collages, there is room for the addition of new pieces. These pieces play a role in changing the composition of the collage. They can spur re-ordering, fill gaps, or serve as connectors between disparate pieces. There is a place for them, regardless of how different or similar they may be and regardless of how much time has passed.

NOTES
Allen, Chadwick. 2012. Trans-Indigenous: Methodologies for Global Native Literary Studies. University of Minnesota Press.
Tuck, Eve, and K. Wayne Yang. 2012. "Decolonization Is Not a Metaphor." Decolonization: Indigeneity, Education & Society 1 (1). http://decolonization.org/index.php/des/article/view/18630.

introduction

JEFF CORNTASSEL, TAIAIAKE ALFRED,
NOELANI GOODYEAR-KAʻŌPUA, HOKULANI AIKAU,
NOENOE SILVA, AND DEVI MUCINA, EDS.

THIS BOOK PROJECT came out of powerful collaborations with Indigenous peoples across the Pacific. Since 2006, we have held a series of international exchanges between the faculty and students of Indigenous Governance (IGOV) at the University of Victoria and the Indigenous Politics Program (UHIP) at the University of Hawaiʻi, Mānoa. The partnership and exchange grew out of an affinity IGOV and UHIP share: both programs are focused on a critical praxis of Indigenous political studies that aims to challenge and transform relations of domination that continue to inflict myriad harms on Indigenous communities and lands/waterways. Over the years, our exchanges have evolved into experiential, land and water-based, community-engaged endeavors. By 2011, we were taking our students to work directly with communities engaged in land-reclamation and cultural revitalization struggles in our respective locations.

In 2015 we came together on Oʻahu to engage in land and water-based cultural practices and to strategize around future mobilizations for community resurgence. We organized our time together around the theme, "Piko: A Convergence of Resurgence." The Kanaka Maoli word, piko, has several meanings, including the navel on a human body, the summit of a mountain, or other places of convergence. As we talked about the piko that grounds us, a Hawaiian student, Andre Perez, talked about the ways we might think of people, places and practices, as piko. These "three P's" became the organizing structure for this book.

Several questions emerged from our 2015 gathering: What is your center? How will your ancestors recognize you? And how will the land and water recognize you in terms of your relationships to place? Finally, how do your everyday actions reflect your relationships with people, places and practices? Often daily actions are overlooked during discussions of community resurgence and self-determination movements. By looking more closely at everyday acts of resurgence, we can identify and better understand ways that Indigenous peoples renew and regenerate relationships with lands, waters, cultures, and communities. These daily convergences of people, places and practices help us envision life beyond the state and honor the relationships that foster community health and well-being. As Anishinaabe scholar Leanne Simpson states, "Resurgence cannot occur in isolation."[1]

Focusing on everydayness helps make visible the often unseen or unacknowledged actions that embody Indigenous nationhood. As Kwakwaka'wakw scholar Sarah Hunt and Cindy Holmes point out, "While large-scale actions such as rallies, protests and blockades are frequently acknowledged as sites of resistance, the daily actions undertaken by individual Indigenous people, families, and communities often go unacknowledged but are no less vital to decolonial processes."[2] These intimate spaces of home and family are critical sites of resurgence and nationhood. They demonstrate how responsibilities are grounded in our relationships and the ways in which we act on them on a daily basis.

Looking more closely at everyday acts of resurgence also gives us a deeper understanding of gendered relationships and how they drive resurgence movements. As Hunt and Holmes explain, it is in the everyday that "we connect these relational decolonial processes to queer, Two-Spirit and trans solidarity, resistance to heteronormativity and cisnormativity, locating these intersections in practices of decolonizing and queering the intimate geographies of the family and the home."[3] Additionally, according to Arvin, Tuck, and Morrill, when discussing decolonizing praxis, "We are arguing that there cannot be feminist thought and theory without Native feminist theory. The experiences and intellectual contributions of Indigenous women are not on the margins; we have been an invisible presence in the center, hidden by the gendered logics of settler colonialism for over 500 years."[4] Within these intimate spaces we see how fatherhood and motherhood are practiced, including other-mothering and other-fathering, and ways that heteropatriarchy and colonial constructions of gender are challenged.

Finally, everydayness allows us to see Indigenous relationality in action. By observing the everyday actions of Indigenous peoples, we gain insights into how extended kinship networks operate in ways that subvert colonial nuclear family structures. Indigenous nations and communities are strengthened and perpetuated by the everyday actions that express and nurture their relationships to lands, waters, language, sacred living histories, and the natural world. Everydayness reveals the choices we make on a daily basis to engage with our lands, cultures and communities. These seemingly small actions are significant in informing both the micro and macro processes of community resurgence. Resurgence also entails a consciousness of being in a daily struggle to regain rebellious dignity. We are interested in how these transformational moments regenerate and invigorate Indigenous nationhood as well as our community and individual health and well-being. While rallies, protests, and other publicized events are often viewed as catalysts for change, it is these quiet, transformational, intimate actions that occur on a daily basis in ways that are seen and unseen that form the basis for revolutionary shifts.

Ultimately, this edited volume is a project grounded in love – love for our land, water, families, clans, communities, ceremonies, sacred histories, and languages, which form our center or piko. The authors who contributed are part of the larger ʻohana or family that we have fostered across the Pacific to write from their hearts and make their work accessible to a more general audience. Our challenge to each author was to write in 1,500 words or less, with little jargon, and with ten citations or less, in order to embody their lived expressions of everydayness. This resulted in twenty-two powerful works that challenge our ways of looking at people, places and practices in an everyday context.

NOTES

[1] Simpson, Leanne (2011). *Dancing On Our Turtle's Back: Stories of Nishnaabeg Re-Creation, Resurgence and a New Emergence.* Winnipeg: Arbeiter Ring, p. 69.

[2] Hunt, Sarah and Cindy Holmes (2015). "Everyday Decolonization: Living a Decolonizing Queer Politics." *Journal of Lesbian Studies.* 19(2): 154-172.

[3] Hunt and Holmes, "Everyday Decolonization," p. 158.

[4] Arvin, Maile, Eve Tuck, and Angie Morrill (2013). "Decolonizing Feminism: Challenging Connections between Settler Colonialism and Heteropatriarchy." *Feminist Formations.* 25(1): 8-34

Lawa Ku'u Lei

KĪHEI DE SILVA

AUTHOR'S NOTE: What follows are my opening words at the 35th annual Holomua ka No'eau, a 2015 concert of Hawaiian music and hula performed by my wife's hālau hula, Hālau Mōhala 'Ilima. The hula we do, on this day and every day, is not the brand of coconut-bra-ed, sarong-clad wiggles still so often associated with "Hawai'i" and "Aloha". It is the grounded, fierce, stately hula of our grandmothers, and of their grandmother's grandmothers. The everyday-ness of resurgence requires us 'ōiwi to persist - to continue to do, say, grow, and dance that which our lāhui always has. Its desire for a surge of support and resistance asks that we also, on occasion, reach out and explain why we do what we do. "Hula", "Aloha", and the Hawaiian "Lei" have suffered much co-optation and attempted assimilation at the hands of colonizers and capitalists. Our continued survival as kānaka maoli will depend on our youth's willingness and ability to see through the false reflections of ourselves that the colonizer's mirror shows us, and on their stubbornness in maintaining our connections with land and lāhui cherished by our people's true practices and attitudes.

Kīhei de Silva
Holomua Ka Noʻeau
March 14, 2015

MY MOM DIED IN FEBRUARY 1987. My dad, my brother, and I took her ashes back to Hōnaunau and scattered them in the ocean at Kapuaʻi. I left a lei maile floating over the spot and watched it travel out to sea as we walked back to our car. My memory of that departing lei inspired "He Inoa no Piʻilani," a song that I wrote with Moon Kauakahi. Its third verse asks us to "huli aku nānā i ka lei maile / Lana i ke ala loa o ka wāwae ehu" -- "turn and pay attention to the lei maile floating on the path of fading, misty footsteps."

We were still trying to come to grips with Mom's death when April arrived and it was time for Merrie Monarch. At about 5 o'clock in the morning of the day of our flight to Hilo, we heard a bang on the door and my brother Kauka called up to me, "Bones ... Bones." Bones is one of my nicknames from small kid time. I went downstairs and found Kauka standing outside, rumpled, crazy-eyed, and carrying a lei maile bunched up in his hands. My brother is the haka in our family; that doesn't mean he does the haka, he's not Maori; it means that he is the "shelf," the one on whom our guardians sit, the one who sees and hears stuff, the one who gets dream visits. "Bones," he tells me, "Mom said to give you this lei."

There was a movie that came out in 2015 called Aloha, and its very "native" cast includes Bradley Cooper, Emma Stone, Rachel MacAdams, and Bill Murray. Bradley Cooper is especially "authentic" in a segment of the movie's trailer that looks like a U.S. military welcoming ceremony at Hickam Field: there are Royal Guardsmen standing at attention in their white Kalākaua-period helmets, the American flag is waving, soldiers are saluting, a couple of shirtless brown guys – also standing at attention – look like they might be dressed in malo... and then the camera comes to rest on "Mr. Sexy Pants," Bradley Cooper who is wearing a vibrant lei maile over his grey T-shirt and flight jacket. I can't wait to see all of Aloha so that I can learn the story of his lei. I wonder if his crazy brother gave it to him; I wonder if it evokes a mother, a hula guardian, and a mele inoa.

Maile is a plant form, a kinolau, of Laka, the guardian deity of hula. The lei maile makes visible its wearer's deep connection to Laka; it speaks of an umbilical cord relationship between child, mother, and mothers' mother, between these kānaka and cloud, rain, forest, leaf, flower, and stream; it is an expression of ke aloha 'āina, of an abiding love for the living land from which we descend. When I see these lei, my ears ring with: "huli aku nānā i ka lei maile," and with:

Eia au, e Laka mai uka
E Laka mai kai
O ho'oulu
'O ka maile hihi i ka wao
'O Laka 'oe
'O ke akua i ke kuahu nei – lā
E ho'i, e ho'i mai a noho i kou kahu.

You will only see two lei maile in tonight's event. Two maile shared at different times in the program by five, very closely connected hula people: by me, Māpuana, Kahikina, Kapalai, and Puakenamu. When Holomua is over, we'll take these maile home with us, and tomorrow morning, I will drape them on the stones that watch over the reinterment site of our iwi kupuna, our ancestors, in the parking lot of the new Target Store in Kailua.

A lei of maile ordered from your favorite Maunakea Street florist will cost from $40 to $60. Twenty-five dancers on a Merrie Monarch stage on Friday night, will then be wearing at least a thousand dollars worth of lei maile. More often than not, maile isn't enough for today's heaped-up, lei nu'a look; so we add three strands of lei 'ilima for fullness and that oh-so-necessary pop of color: three strands at 20-30 dollars a strand times, twenty-five dancers and you're now looking at a minimum of 1500 more dollars on that MM stage. And we have yet to tally-in the requisite head, wrist, and ankle lei, preferably made of palapalai fern and lehua blossoms; most top shelf lei-makers will charge 100 dollars for the complete set. 25 x 100 = twenty-five hundred dollars. So now we are looking a minimum of 5,000 dollars of lei dancing around the Kanaka'ole Stadium stage for seven minutes. It can easily be 7,000 dollars, which is a thousand a minute. As Kapalai said when I read this tally sheet to her, "Dad, they're still naked. You haven't accounted for the cost of costumes, hair, nails, and make–up."

There are a few hālau who refuse to buy into this madness – hālau whose dancers make their own lei, sew their own costumes, do their own primping as best they can in the belief that you aren't really a dancer, an 'ōlapa, if you can't take care of all your kuleana. But these are rarely the top-scoring, trophy-winning hālau, especially in the Miss Hula and wahine divisions of the festival. The MM score-sheet awards a maximum of ten points for the quality and significance of the dancers' lei, and assigns a max of ten more points for grooming, and ten more for costume. This accounts for thirty points of a possible 125 – about twenty-five percent of the total score in a competition whose winners are often decided by tie-breakers or by margins of one or two points.

If you are just a wee bit cynical, you might conclude that trophy-driven hālau cannot afford to lose points on the look of their dancers; you might conclude that victory is often a matter of budget, that winning scores are often a reflection of how much a hālau is willing and able to spend on florist and lei-maker, on seamstress, hairstylist, manicurist, and make-up artist.

I have a quote. It's from Auntie Marie MacDonald in her 1978 publication Ka Lei, The Leis of Hawaii. It reminds us of old-school thinking about the relationship between mele, hula dancer, and lei.

Dancers were careful not to over-adorn themselves because the important thing in hula was the telling of the story and the singing of praises with body movement. The words of the story were not muffled by an excessive number of lei. One for the head and one for the neck were sufficient for enhancing the story telling.

In old-school thinking, the dancer's lei is significant because it is made by the dancer from materials that the dancer has gathered. In old-school thinking the lei of the dancer is dedicated to Laka, the guardian of hula, who then inspires the dancer with understanding, connection, and excellence. We are reminded by old-school thinkers like Auntie Marie and Tutu Kawena Pukui that: "Puʻupuʻu lei, pali i ka ʻāʻī. An imperfect lei is made beautiful by the one who makes, dedicates, and wears it.

We do our best to be-old school in what we make and wear. Yes, we will order lei maile for MM this year, but from someone who knows the value of careful, sustainable picking; from a steward, not a trampler. We will have our ʻauana dresses made by a dress-maker who was Auntie Maiki's dress-maker, and who is now almost family. But everything else of ours will be very in- house: tops and pāʻū that we've sewn ourselves; lei that we pick ourselves from plants that we ourselves take care of; lei that we make ourselves, pack in coolers ourselves, take to Hilo ourselves, tend-to in Hilo ourselves, put on and take off ourselves. Lei that we will return, ourselves – when the dancing is over – to their home in the land to which we are forever attached.

Tonight's concert is titled "Kuʻu Pua, Kuʻu Lei Aloha" – My Flower, My Beloved Lei" – and it will feature five oli, eight hula ʻōlapa, and fifteen hula ʻauana, all of them composed for various flowers and the beloved lei into which they are fashioned. My daughters Kahikina and Kapalai came up with this theme and with most of the twenty-eight mele that we'll share with you in the next three hours. I myself wanted to put on a concert called "E Pāka Kākou" in honor of our Mayor's new and brilliantly named program for recruiting community volunteers to help fix-up our county parks. The word Pāka is a Hawaiianization of the English word park as in "beach park"; so "E Pāka Kākou" means "Let's all park" in the same kind of grammatical context as "Let's all post office," or "Let's all mortuary," or "Let's all bakery." The words paka and kapaka, without the initial ā -emphasis, can also mean tobacco, so "E Paka Kākou" translates to "Let's all tobacco." I thought that this would surely make for a great and hilarious concert theme: we could dance "Ala Moana Pāka," "Haleʻiwa Pāka," "Home Kapaka," and my favorite "Hoʻā i ka Paka Lōlō." I thought this, but I held my tongue, knowing full well that I would get the ix-nay on the aka-pay from our young master minds.

Actually, pua and lei make for a pretty good theme, especially when you look at it from Mary Kawena Pukui's point of view as expressed in her 1964 essay "Aspects of the Word Lei." She reminds us that pua are not limited to flower blossoms; pua can include grasses, seaweeds, leaves, fronds, vines, shells, seeds, feathers, children, sweethearts, and the citizens of a nation. She reminds us that grandchildren who wrap their arms lovingly around our necks are called "lei moʻopuna." She reminds us that our cherished grandparents are called "lei hulu kūpuna." She reminds us that a lei can be a chant or song that is given to an esteemed person with or without an accompanying flower lei. When the lei of flowers fades away, the lei of words remains.

Kawena doesn't say it, but I think that years can also be thought of as pua. Holomua ka Noʻeau is, tonight, a lei of thirty-five amazing years. Our return to the Merrie Monarch Festival next month will be a lei strung from the flowers of thirty-seven consecutive years. And Hālau Mōhala ʻIlima itself is now an unbroken lei of thirty-nine years. In my mind, a lei of years is very much like this other lei that I'm wearing, a lei hala. A lei hala embraces all that is hala – all that is gone but still cherished, all that, like years and memories, is gathered up, strung, and held close.

In my mind, our hālau of blossoming ʻilima is still thriving after all these years because it is sheltered by hala and maile. I try to be the kahu of what is past but cherished; Mapu is kumu of what is generative and ongoing. Together we have managed to stand guard over the place in which our lei ʻāpiki, our beautiful, mischievous ʻilima can blossom and shine.

Ka hala o kai Maile aʻo uka

Kui aʻe kāua Lawa kuʻu lei.

[note: from Daniel Kaopio's mele "Ke ʻAla o ka Rose."]

Hala of the seaside, maile of the uplands, when we join together, our lei is complete.

NOTES

[1] The Merrie MonarchFestival is a non-profit organization that honors the legacy left by King David Kalākaua, who inspired the perpetuation of our traditions, native language and arts. More details available at: http://merriemonarch.com/drupal/index.php

[2] It should be noted that I shortened this prayer chant.

[3] It should be noted that I edited this passage.

people

~NIBWAAKAAWIN
(wisdom)

JANA-RAE YERXA

i asked her

'grandma would you be okay

sitting in ceremony with me

even if i didn't wear a skirt?'

without hesitation

and love in her eyes

she said 'yes.'

...then continued

'whatever you do

has to have meaning for you.'

Resurgence as Relationality

GINA STARBLANKET

INDIGENOUS RESURGENCE CAN TAKE PLACE in a multiplicity of ways in our everyday experiences, in various realms of life and on individual, interpersonal, and institutional levels. Although it occurs in diverse forms and carries different meanings across and within communities, it is generally understood as comprising a process of critically informed action or praxis rather than a body of theory or ideas. Yet as more writers (including the contributors to this volume) engage with questions surrounding the nature, form and implications of different approaches to resurgence, it is becoming increasingly evident that resurgence movements also have a strong theoretical component. This article explores the practical consequences of the way in which Indigenous resurgence is theorized. It begins by reviewing the everyday implications of different ways of conceptualizing resurgence, arguing that they have the potential to circumscribe our movements in ways that can seriously undermine or strengthen their efficacy and success. It explores the limitations of a unitary or fixed approach to resurgence, and advances a relational understanding as more insightful at the level of inquiry and more productive in practice. Ultimately, this chapter examines how political projects that conceptualize resurgence as a relational, dynamic process allow for a more robust, equitable and accessible range of movements than permitted by a static, singular conception.

In contemporary discussions on Indigenous decolonization and resurgence, there has been significant attention in recent years to the limits and contradictions of working towards our political objectives within liberal modes of engagement. Critical Indigenous and post-colonial scholars are increasingly interrogating the emancipatory potential of projects of self-determination that work within state sanctioned legal and political structures, highlighting the ways in which they reproduce the configurations of power they purport to oppose and more importantly, the ways in which they constrain the space for meaningful political dialogue about the future. These critiques have led many Indigenous peoples to move away from asserting our political imperatives within the parameters of rights and recognition circumscribed by settler states. Consequently, we have also seen a resurgence of community organizing and dialogue grounded in our ancestral values, places, knowledges and spirituality. The growth of Indigenous resurgence movements is evident across the globe, and can be seen everywhere from local community initiatives to international networks such as the Indigenous Nationhood Movement.[1] As these movements continue to gain currency, it is vital that we reflect upon the ways in which they are being conceptualized and characterized to ensure that they remain adaptable to new contexts and challenges, but also attentive to the needs of all community members.

Conventional definitions of the concept of resurgence describe it a form of awakening or revival after a period of dormancy. In Indigenous contexts it also carries a particular cultural and political meaning, referring to a course of action geared towards the revitalization of our traditional lifeways. The intent is for these efforts to contribute to the restoration of our ability to practice the relationships with people, places and practices that were disrupted through colonialism. The renewal of these connections necessarily involves confronting the impacts of colonialism and engaging in resistance to its contemporary manifestations, however resurgence also involves broadening our focus beyond the realm of decolonization. While the discourse of decolonization serves an important diagnostic purpose, resurgence involves the healing and strengthening of our communities on our own terms. This is a tall order, the actualization of which may seem daunting when we consider the extent of structural change required to fully achieve these reconnections. However, thinking of resurgence as an ongoing way of life rather than something to be accomplished all at once can help give it traction by directing our attention to the ways we can engage in resurgence within the existing relationships we inhabit. The Cree term kîwêhtahiwê, which means "to take others home with one" can provide important inspiration in thinking about resurgence as a fundamentally relational process; in this phrase, the word home embodies the concept of resurgence, which we engage in collectively through actions that are geared towards going home.

Conceptualizing resurgence in a relational way directs our attention to the significant role that our everyday interactions play in defining and pursuing our political objectives and priorities. It helps us recognize the transformative possibilities that exist in the processes of exploration and learning that we experience within our relationships. It locates resurgence within the everyday choices we make about the way in which we live our lives and the conversations that we choose to have, or not to have, with those around us. A relational approach also has the potential to demonstrate that change is not limited to large-scale actions that occur within the realm of social justice organizing. Instead, it positions resurgence as a dynamic and ongoing process that is constantly changing and comprises a multiplicity of everyday relations. While resurgence certainly requires change to macro structures of power, it can be engaged in small but meaningful ways in various realms of life. When we contemplate resurgence as a set of living and evolving ideas and practices that are open to dialogue and reinterpretation, we gain a more intimate understanding of the significance of acts of resurgence that can take place within our relations with our family and friends, within our relations with ideas and knowledge, as well as our relationship with ourselves.

Because it is through our interactions with our environments that we learn most about ourselves and those we share our existence with, our relationships have the biggest potential to act as sites of change and imagination. The relational nature of processes of learning and transformation is particularly evident to me when I reflect upon how my relationship with my daughter has driven me to live in a more balanced and sustainable way. By sustainable, I am referring to the maintenance of a healthy physical environment for her and for future generations to live in, but also the act of living in a healthy way so that I can be a positive presence in her life for as long as possible. This has involved fundamental change in my day-to-day interactions as well as my broader long-term goals and plans. It has not simply impacted the way I understand my responsibilities towards our environments, but also towards those around us.

My relationship with my daughter has taught me how to be humble, to stay grounded, and to have confidence in my decisions while also recognizing opportunities for learning and critical introspection. It has taught me patience and how to engage with people based on where they are at in their learning. It has taught me that inhabiting a relationship of care for others does not mean sacrificing care for the self, but that the two go hand-in-hand. While these were all notions that I was committed to prior to becoming a mother, I didn't fully understand how to live them in my everyday interactions. The relationship itself is what inspired me to integrate these previously theoretical qualities into my day-to-day actions and consciousness. Similar transformative possibilities exist within all relationships, and understanding their significance can help provide important insight into the ways in which our interconnectedness is vital to multiple forms of individual and community change and empowerment.

As Indigenous peoples, our capacity to survive and to live sustainably over time has been dependent on the way in which we understand our relationships with our environments and other beings that we share our lives with. By seeing ourselves as co-constituted through and directly responsible to these relationships, we have managed to learn from our environments and adapt our ways of being to new developments and challenges. When the ecosystems we inhabit are disrupted, invaded, or changed, we have always found new means of survival by adjusting to the circumstances or challenges we have been faced with. The configurations of our lives have been context-dependent and dynamic, in large part due to the underlying relationality that characterizes our worldviews and spirituality. Embodying this relationality through our future ways of living can represent a powerful form of resurgence. It subverts the individualism that characterizes contemporary liberal society, while honoring and carrying forward the way of life of those who came before us.

Instead of understanding resurgence as an individuated set of qualities, characteristics or commitments, a relational approach positions it as an ongoing and incremental process of change and consciousness-raising. This process does not occur in isolation, but is co-constituted through our relations with other beings, places, ideas and practices. By broadening our focus beyond independent units (such as individuals or collectives) as the primary actors, we stand to gain a better understanding of the inner workings of processes of resurgence, which in turn might allow us to strategize and engage more effectively. A relational understanding of resurgence can also enable us to reflect critically and avoid the potential limitations and implications of a unitary or static approach. When our approach to resurgence results in the production of a normative or singular discourse, it breeds a conformism that has the potential to re-inscribe the forms of hierarchy and discipline it is intended to transcend. It also severely limits the scope of dialogue around the range of ways in which our political imperatives may be pursued. We then run the risk of being resubordinated through the very discourse that is intended to reinforce our boundaries with Western legal and political systems. A relational approach has the potential to mitigate these risks by demonstrating that there is no fixed structure or formula defining resurgence movements, but that they are constantly changing, contingent and culturally produced.

In discussing everyday approaches to resurgence, it might therefore be worthwhile to discuss the possibility that there are no specific qualities characterizing true or authentic forms of resurgence, as these are far too reductive to understand the ways in which acts of resurgence are co-constituted in our everyday relations. Rather than defining the fundamental elements that are constitutive of an authentic or traditional vision of resurgence, we might stand to gain more insight by examining the ways in which our multiple everyday interactions have the potential to be acts of resurgence. Because relationships drive the growth, change and transformation that occur within resurgence movements, analyses of the relations that connect ideas, people, places, and practices within these movements are vital to their viability and continuation.

NOTES
[1] http://nationsrising.org

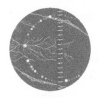

Renewal

JEFF CORNTASSEL

I DREAMED ABOUT HER BEFORE SHE WAS BORN. While living in Virginia, I was going through some rough times, and at one of my lowest points, when I didn't think I could handle the stress anymore, I dreamt of a beautiful little girl playing in a field. I was flying overhead, hovering over the field. The girl had long, light brown hair and I knew she was my daughter. The geography of the place in my dream was different from Virginia, so I figured we must have moved to a different place – one where everything was really lush and green. That dream came to me about five years before she was born and lifted my spirits at a time when I felt beaten down...it was a moment of renewal. *Atsehisodiyi.*

Settler society tends to think of renewal in terms of consumerist ideals – escaping life's challenges with spa days, shopping, vacations, entertainment, all of that. For me, the most powerful aspects of renewal come from daily spiritual obligations and actions promoting community consciousness. The dream reminds me of our accountability to future generations...to those generations yet unborn. How will future generations recognize me as Cherokee? Or any of us as being from a particular Indigenous nation? More importantly, what are my responsibilities to future generations? These are challenges that we take up in the everyday – those often unseen, unacknowledged actions that renew our peoplehood and generate community resurgence. And how did I recognize her as being my daughter? I just knew. You sense it in your gut as that feeling of belonging and recognition washes over you. It's that sense of belonging, or community cama- raderie that sparks renewal. This extends beyond fatherhood, motherhood, and well beyond those artificial boundaries that we construct around relations, such as 1st, 2nd or 3rd cousins. Such artificial distinctions can distance us from each other and obscure the depth of our familial sense of belonging. At the end of the day as Indigenous nations, we all belong to each other. *Digadatseli'i.*

My daughter is older now and she still likes to hear about how I dreamed about her before she was born. To draw on a word used extensively by our Kanaka Maoli brothers and sisters, she is my *piko*, my center or umbilical cord; she is the convergence of the people, place and practices that piko represents. After she was born the nurses saved the birth cord and placenta for me in the refrigerator. I froze it for several months while thinking of a plan for how to return it to Cherokee territory and bury it in our family territory near Westville, Oklahoma. I wanted to motivate her to go home and feel what it's like to walk among our ancestors...to breathe in and connect with the land so deeply that you can't imagine your life without it. When my daughter was older, I showed her where it was buried in Oklahoma, and she remembers. Through a process of renewal (retelling and regenerating this story and actions that go with it), she embodies her relational responsibilities. This is where people, place and prac- tices converge. *Piko.*

When speaking of everydayness, we should be careful to not romanticize these actions. They are often thankless. Anyone who raises children knows that the daily realities of parenting can be exhausting and frustrating at times. To a single parent struggling to put food on the table, everyday life might seem over- whelming. But everyday acts of resurgence persist amidst these hardships and occur despite ongoing colonial and neo-liberal impositions on our lives. They can be very simple practices that appear mundane. Ever since she was two or so, I've asked Leila three questions pretty much everyday: Osiyo Tohi'tsu (hello, how are you)?; Gado usdi gawonihisdi hewoni (what language are you speak- ing)?; and, Tsalagi hiyosgitsu (are you a Tsalagi warrior)?

Embedded in the word Osiyo (the first question), which is often translated as "hello", is the word "osi", which means being upright, forward-facing, and ex- isting on a single point of balance.[1] When I speak to my daughter in Cherokee, I'm really asking her if she's aligned and balanced with the unhurried pace of nature. Just one part of one word in the Cherokee language carries so much with it. I'm also ensuring that Cherokee is spoken on a daily basis. These deeper understandings of language are symptomatic of everyday acts of resurgence that might be overlooked by a casual observer. These questions attempt to breathe life into the language, even in a small, seemingly insignificant way. They covertly function as unseen acts of renewal. After all, resurgence is about renewing, nurturing and re-awakening those relationships that promote individual and community health and well-being. In this sense, how she responds to these questions signifies her commitment to them. We start with these basic questions and continue to build on them. In doing so, we're also giving breath to the unhurried pace of nature and ultimately challenging western notions of time and place. *Osi.*

How we convey Indigenous values and practices to future generations is sometimes just as important as what we're teaching. When a child asks why something is done a certain way, how do you respond? Do you say "because it's traditional", "it's how we do things" or just "because"? Those are unsatisfying answers for anyone to hear, whether as a child or adult. After all, community 'traditions' are constantly changing and evolving. Future generations demand better answers to their questions as they weigh their obligations to re-interpret Cherokee teachings alongside a renewal of their commitments to them. It's not enough to claim something is traditional – it should be embodied in your everyday actions and follow an inherent Indigenous logic. Renewal is strengthened through reinterpretation and reconnection.

When I was visiting the ahupua'a of Kahana (O'ahu, Hawai'i) in March 2015, I saw a sign urging Kanaka Maoli people to "Educate to perpetuate". It is through our everyday actions that we seek to restore and perpetuate Indigenous peoples, places, and practices. This can be tricky, even when learning Indigenous languages in our own communities. We have to be careful what we're perpetuating. I recently spoke with a parent who was pulling her child out of an Indigenous language immersion kindergarten class. When I asked why, the parent said that the Indigenous teacher was just merely reinforcing a western way of learning and her child no longer enjoyed learning the language. This is a heartbreaking story but not that uncommon. Education that reproduces the alienating and competitive processes of colonial classrooms can be incredibly harmful, even within an Indigenous context. Humor, patience, and Indigenous pedagogies are crucial to inspiring future generations to educate to perpetuate. As Nishnaabekwe scholar Leanne Betasamosake Simpson states so powerfully, "Resurgence is our original instruction."[2]

The Cherokee notion of leadership starts with a person having a vision or dream. That person begins to embody that vision by putting it into everyday practice. While implementing it, the person also has a responsibility to makes that vision understandable to other people through her/his words and actions. After gaining this experience, the person offers some direction for people to mobilize around that vision. In short this is leadership by example that is common to most Indigenous nations. When speaking of what decolonization entailed during the 2011 UHIP/IGOV exchange, Kanaka Maoli Ph.D. student Kahikina de Silva pointed out that decolonizing praxis entails moving beyond performance and/or symbolic gestures to everyday practices of decolonization.[3] These everyday actions give life to our dreams and visions. My daughter embodies renewal and resurgence for me. The practice of speaking the Cherokee language at home is how I mobilize the responsibilities that came with my initial dream. It is through these reconnections to people, place, and practices that spiritual revolutions are born and the rebellious dignity of Indigenous nations is proudly renewed.

NOTES

[1] Altman, Heidi and Tom Belt. 2011. "Moving Around in the Room: Cherokee Language, Worldview and Memory" in Margaret Williamson Huber, ed. *Museums and Memory*. Knoxville: Newfound Press, p. 227. Available at: http://newfoundpress.utk.edu//pubs/museums/chp11.pdf

[2] Simpson, Leanne. 2011. *Dancing On Our Turtle's Back: Stories of Nishnaabeg Re-Creation, Resurgence and a New Emergence*. Winnipeg: Arbeiter Ring, p. 66.

[3] de Silva, Kahikina. July 19, 2011. "Pathways to Decolonization" class session, University of Hawai'i Indigenous Politics/Indigenous Governance Program exchange course, IGOV 595: Reclaiming Ćelánen: Land, Water, Governance, University of Victoria, Victoria, British Columbia, Canada.

Relentlessly Coastal

Parenting, Research, and Everyday Resurgence[1]

MICK SCOW

I T IS MY DEEPEST DESIRE that my children are given the opportunity to live a more Indigenous life than I did. It is for this reason that I've included my children in my research, both academic and informal. To do so I've had to transform the ways in which I conceive of and partake in research. I came to understand research as a process that allow us, *as* Indigenous peoples, to better understand our place within our communities. It is a journey of relating to, participating with, and coming to understand all of our relations. Research, as such, entails an active reconnection with the forces of the universe that colonial rule has sought to separate us from. For our family, this has meant rooting our research within traditional philosophies and within traditional webs of relations. By undertaking research of this nature, we are committing to the reassertion and rebuilding of traditional knowledge from its roots, its fundamental principles. We do this as parents with the hope that we will raise Indigenous intellectuals "who think within the conceptual meanings of our languages, who embody our stories, [and] traditions"[2]. In this respect, research has becoming more than just an academic practice. Research is an everyday practice of living in a longer Indigenous present.

I do not want my children to grow up as disconnected from our communities as I did. Cultures of resistance are built upon everyday acts dedicated to the revitalization of Indigenous families, communities, and nations. Revolution, in the sense of a wheel turning, is propelled by small, everyday acts, like raising children in a good way. As Corntassel reminds us, these acts can be lost in the broader discussions of resurgence. They are the unseen acts of renewal that unite long histories of struggle. They are meant to reclaim, restore, and reinvigorate.

As parents, we are responsible for creating the political and cultural contexts that will allow our kids to thrive *as* Indigenous children. Part of this has been a commitment to reside upon, as well as reestablish and maintain culturally relevant relationships with *S'olh Temexw*, the lands and waters that nourish our territories. We visit the ocean near our home as often as we can, giving thanks for all that it provides. We escape the city by hiding amongst the trees and visiting our relatives, sharing food and stories, experiencing daily the relationships that I missed out on as a child.

For me, this is what resurgence looks (and feels) like in my daily actions. Resurgence is about creating Indigenous worlds within the spaces that we dwell in our day-to-day lives. It is about parenting in a good way. It is about *uy'skwuluwun*, about being of good heart and good mind. I've learned that good relations require the presence of *uy'skwuluwun.* Growing up there were times in my life where my fathers just weren't there. For this reason, I've approached fatherhood with the belief that my presence is one of the greatest gifts I can give my children. Just being there for my kids is so important to me. However, I've also learned that my being there, my physical presence, alone is not enough. Our relationships depend on the presence of love.

Hwunitumology and parenting

We currently live in a world out of balance. We live in a world of "too much". There are so many distractions at our disposal. We get lost in our work, searching for jobs and for meaning. We wander the world inside our phones and this too muchness conspires to make being present very difficult. Sadly, it often takes conscious effort to live in the moment. Instead, we are left lost, wandering, and hungry.

The Hul'qumi'num term that we use the most to refer to non-Indigenous peoples, to refer to the settlers who came north into our territories during and following the Gold Rushes of the 1850s, is *hwunitum*, which loosely translates as "the hungry people". These miners came empty-handed and they were starving. Our people took pity on these men, bringing them into the community where they were clothed, sheltered and fed, according to our traditions. However, no amount of salmon could suppress their appetites, for what they craved was gold, what they craved was land. Since the arrival of the *hwunitum*, Indigenous nations along the coast have been under attack.

In turn, my academic work has focused on developing *hwunitumology*, which is the study of colonial mentalities as they've manifested on *S'olh Temexw*, Coast Salish homelands. This land-based approach focuses not only on settler colonialism but also on the viability of Indigenous perspectives it seeks to eliminate and hold up alternative ways of seeing and being in the world, relying upon the conceptual meanings of our languages and stories. As such, I see *hwunitumology* as a culturally and politically relevant methodological tool for conducting research on *S'olh Temexw*, in both academic and community settings. Ultimately, *hwunitumology* is premised on an ongoing sovereign Indigenous presence on *S'olh Temexw*, including within urban settings, such as occupied Victoria and Vancouver.

This methodological approach has proven tremendously powerful in how we parent our children. When my daughter was young, we needed a narrative to answer many of the questions she had about the world. Eventually, I decided to share a number of *hwunitum* stories with her, telling her about a group of hungry people who have caused a great imbalance in our homelands. Rather than being a racialized term, I felt *hwunitum* was an ideal phrase because it serves to highlight colonial mentalities that both colonizer and colonized have come to embody. The insatiable hunger, both physical and spiritual, of the *hwunitum* went a long way in helping her come to understand the injustices that she saw all around her. She has taken ownership of these stories, referring to the *hwunitum* as "the greedy people," telling stories and asking questions that help her better understand her place in this world. As a co-creator, she has shown me that there is room for her, and for all children, within Indigenous research.

Making research an everyday practice has allowed me, as a parent, to be much more present in my kids' lives. Living in the moment allows us to connect with our children on their terms, whether being silly, hugging and cuddling one another, crawling around as kittens, or catching them when they fall ("skateboarder fall down, skateboarder get up" is a mantra in our home). This emotional presence has been a challenge for me as a father. Our children have taught me to be open and honest, to be vulnerable in ways I've never allowed myself to be. I've had to learn that it is okay to be upset, to be disappointed or frustrated – we all have these moments and being a good parent isn't necessarily about avoiding these emotions and reactions. However, I've also had to learn to reconnect, rather than detach myself, an expression of dissent I learned from my childhood. We disagree and we argue, but then we come together again. I apologize for my actions, allowing them to hold me accountable, and I am always so overwhelmed by how forgiving children can be.

Hwunitum mentalities appear as though they are dead to love and the only way we are going to break free from these corrosive ways of thinking and being is to resurrect our nations by means of spiritual awakening. This begins with our families and how we choose to parent our children. A commitment to a spiritual life, to love, requires conscious practice and presence. This sort of resurgence requires a willingness to unite the way we think with the way we act. It requires the type of integrity that *uy'skwuluwun* demands. We must also think and behave in ways that honour the principles of inter-being and interconnectedness, which *nutsa maat* embodies. We need to return to the gathering, sharing, and generous traditions of our ancestors and we must do this together, as a community of Indigenous nations. Liberation from *hwunitum* mentalities is a collective process and it requires ongoing, coordinated action. This politicization of *Hwulmuhw* principles of *nutsa maat* and *uy'skwuluwun* is often absent but are certainly needed in both our resistance and resurgence struggles.

Coming together to feast, our children beaming, ducking and diving between the legs of parents, aunties and uncles, who watch on with swelling hearts, we see the seeds of resurgence. Their laughter fills the air with the sweetest of sounds, uniting us in our love for each other and the diverse communities that we carry with us. It is in these moments that my ancestors would recognize me. In sharing stories, whether origin stories of our homelands or stories of resistance and resurgence, both past and present, we teach our children that Indigenous narratives are not just about oppression. Our stories are a testament to our resistance, resilience, and resurgence as Indigenous peoples. These convergences of resurgences have pushed us to continue to do what we do in spite of colonial attempts to reframe us. All of these events, whether fishing or harvesting from our homelands, feasting together, or raising our children are convergences of stories, experiences, and love. We come together with good hearts and good minds. We come together to renew and rejoice in our relationships. In an everyday kind of sense, this is Indigenous resurgence in action. It is our responsibility to work towards these moments and make them last, so that we can live a longer, Indigenous present.

NOTES

[1] My title, *Relentlessly Coastal*, is based on a phrase coined by Nuu-chah-nulth scholar and activist, Chaw-win-is, found in Sarah Hunt's dissertation, "Witnessing the Colonialscape: Lighting the Intimate Fires of Indigenous Legal Pluralism" (Simon Fraser University, 2014), p. 181. This phrase has resonated with me, informing the way I see myself as coastal, as Kwakwaka'wakw and Snuneymuxw. As Chaw-win-is states: "no one gets to decide who we are. We get to decide who we are".

[2] Simpson, Leanne. 2011. *Dancing on Our Turtle's Back: Stories of Nishnaabeg Re-Creation, Resurgence, and a New Emergence*. Winnipeg: Arbeiter Ring Publishing, p. 31.

Decolonizing Indigenous Fatherhood

Understanding Our Masculinity beyond Imposed Meaning

DEVI MUCINA

T O START THIS ENGAGEMENT, I would like to give you a specific contextualize notion of Indigenous fatherhood as interpreted from the relational paradigm of Ubuntuism. This Indigenous African paradigm of Ubuntuism was first given to me through our Indigenous African oral structure of communication. Given that I left Zimbabwe at the age of 21 and have lived in Canada for 25 years, I have had to nurture my Ubuntu scholarship through centering my childhood memories of Ubuntu teachings, while also researching texts as a way of addressing the gaps in my memories or as a way of gaining new knowledge. In doing this, I have engaged through dialogue with other Indigenous scholars who center their personal, political and spiritual realities of relational connectivity, which embodies Ubuntuism. Doing this has helped me find new ways to communicate how we as Indigenous peoples matter to each other in the world, while also communicating that Ubuntuism is relational. In our convergent and divergent stories, relational Ubuntu has guided our daily actions of liberating Indigenous fatherhood, which we as Ubuntu cannot talk about without talking about motherhood and other-mothering because in the colonial context and beyond, it is women who have played the largest role in fathering us. It is women, who have reminded us about our roles as fathers and other-fathers. My centering of Indigenous men's fathering and other-fathering as decolonizing everyday actions, is intimately intertwined and connected to women's every day actions of caring and nurturing children. After all, it is the Indigenous African work on mothering and other-mothering by Dr. Wane, which has made me more intentional about how I can nurture and care for our children as an Indigenous man beyond my own biological relational connections.

As I engage you using the Ubuntu relational paradigm, it is important that I convey to you what Ubuntu is; how it relates to you; why it should matter to you; and why it matters to our everydayness. Ubuntu is an Indigenous African philosophical and ethical system of thought, from which definitions of everyday humanness, togetherness and the social politics of difference arises.[1] Ubuntuism can also be viewed as a complex worldsense (beyond privileging the single sense of site as the central sense in knowledge acquisition) that holds in tension the contradictions of trying to highlight our uniqueness as human beings among other human beings. So to engage the everyday politics and tensions of the human condition in a diverse world, the Indigenous worldsense of Ubuntu centers relational reciprocal engagement in the web of life. A good example of this kind of relational reciprocal engagement as guided by Ubuntu is conveyed in how our community of friends in Halifax, Nova Scotia has other- fathered and other-mothered our children as part of the everydayness of childcare. Our friends have babysat so we could get a break from giving childcare to our kids, they have played with our children, educated our children, fed our children, told our children stories and listened to our children's stories. I believe these everyday acts of Ubuntuness are important for decolonizing Indigenous child care and centering men in child care because as Indigenous men we cannot leave all the work of childcare with our women folks. I hope I have made it clear how I use Ubuntuism as the Indigenous paradigm for understanding and exploring individual actions that add to the collective actions of decolonizing fatherhood by contemplating the Indigenous notion of other-fathering through Ubuntuism.

In March 2015, I went to Hawaii for the first time to attend the program exchange between University of Hawaii's Indigenous Politics Program and the University of Victoria's Indigenous Governance program. The titled of this exchange was Piko: Convergence of Resurgence. The first thing that struck me was the strong presence of children and babies at an academic gathering. More impressively, I observed sisters and brothers other-mothering and other-fathering the children and babies as was needed. If the child's biological mother or father was attending to another task, one of the other sisters or brothers automatically stepped in to nurture and attend to the needs of the child. I watched these Indigenous women and men regenerate and decolonize mothering and fathering through their everyday actions of other-mothering and other-fathering. This led me to reflect on the prominent African Indigenous scholar, Dr. Wane's writing on other-mothering. Dr. Wane talks about how other women (and men in some situations) care for children in our communities. In her scholarship on Indigenous African mothering, she communicated that mothering is more than the biological act of creating a child and she informs us that, "Our mothers, aunties, sisters and community mothers carried us on their backs."[2] Dr. Wane has named this community mothering as other-mothering. Meaning, we are all responsible to mother beyond our own biological children. So here I was in Hawai'i at a very important Indigenous Governance gathering and I was wondering if we as Indigenous men were aware that we were other-fathering when we cared for children beyond our own biology. I question what it would mean to Indigenous men to have their caring named as other-fathering? Would other Indigenous men care? Would they see themselves reflected? As I dismiss the importance of other-fathering to Indigenous men, I started to reflect on my own experience.

I was other-mothered and other-fathered, because the colonial project and its governing structures of white supremacy fragmented my family through the creations of colonial state boundaries, colonial reserves as a way for stealing our lands and imposing colonial taxation, which led to forced labour migrations. Under these colonially created realities I was born in Zimbabwe, in the rural lands of Makoni on the colonially created reserve of Chendmuya to Joyce Nyamunda. This makes me thankful to my Shona relatives on my Amai's (mother) side. Without them we would have no life. I am because they are. This is the genealogical blood memory that connects me to my maternal family. Yet our Ubuntu Indigenous traditions dictate that when I am in the Shona territory of Zimbabwe, I am a welcomed familial visitor as my rightful place is with my paternal family according to our Ubuntu traditions. Through my Baba's (father) lineage, I am Maseko Ngoni from LiZulu, which is on the colonial border of Malawi and Mozambique (again we see how colonialism fragmented our Indigenous nations). My Baba is Peter Dee Mucina and my totem is Khomba. Due to high colonial taxes which forced Indigenous Africans to migrate to colonially dominated, white settler spaces, I grew up in Zimbabwe. The colonially created reserve of Chendmuya could not sustain the needs of my family, so my father had to leave his family and go to the city of Harare to find a job as a cheap laborer but his sporadic jobs did not pay him enough to support his growing family. Many years later, my mother reported to me that she did unspeakable things to try and keep us alive, but as hard as she tried she saw her babies die one by one from malnutrition and poverty. Colonially fragmented from each other, Amai and Baba struggled against the colonially imposed poverty, while being isolated from each other. It was inevitable that the colonial created white supremacy governance structure would make them evaluate each other against its colonial expectations of capitalistic accumulation. Not surprising they found each other to be failures in the colonial capitalistic structure of white supremacy. Again my Amai reports that it was around this time period in their lives that my Baba started having psychotic mental health breakdowns.

Fearing that I would die next from malnutrition and poverty, my Amai and her family demanded that my Baba come and take me away. This is how I became the child that was raised by the community. I learned everyday actions of being an Ubuntu family member, like cutting wood, cooking food, cleaning the home, preparing the fields for crops, and caring for younger kids because community members took the time to other-father and other-mother me. I know I was other-fathered by the other Indigenous Ubuntu men who let Baba and I stay with them illegally in the servants' quarters. I was other-fathered by the older Indigenous Ubuntu boy who slept in the phone booth with me because I was scared of being beaten by my own biological father. I was other-fathered by the Indigenous servants at the orphanage who loved and cared for me when I wanted nothing to do with them because they were Black and I wanted the power of white supremacy. I was other-mothered by Ubuntu women that fed me, let me practice caring for a baby with their baby children and I was also other-mothered by White women who educated me on how to survive in a White man's world. Other-father and other-mothering is our last chance as Indigenous communities to decolonize and resist white supremacy and its governing structures of colonial violence, dispossession and capitalistic accumulation. It is disastrous when other-mothering and other-fathering is not done enough, I know because I remember experiencing and seeing the consequence of it in our all boys orphanage in Harare. But let me also communicate how simple everyday other-fathering can also be. When I am out at the park playing with my children and I notice a child being left out, I invite that child to play with us. I have offered hugs, said I love you to other peoples' children, wiped running noses and made time to play soccer with a child who needed just a moment of my time. This is other-fathering, do you remember it? Have you experienced it? Will you help me when I do not know if I am fathering the right way? Can we teach each other this kind of Indigenous resurgence as decolonizing masculinity? Other-fathering is political action that is grounded in relational loving respect. Now that I have reminded you of our Indigenous responsibility to other-father, let us do this work so that we support and work in balance with the hard work being done by Indigenous women. This summer, Nandi and Khumalo, our daughter and son, received so much everyday acts of other-fathering and other-mothering from our community of friends in Halifax, Nova Scotia. They started having a hard time determining, which people were blood family and which people were community family. This is other-fathering and other-mothering done well. Let us share this knowledge with future generations. Now that we are connected by this story, where do I end and you begin, could breath, connect us to the cycle of life, Ubuntu.

NOTES

[1] The definition of Ubuntu that I offer here comes from a more in-depth definition that I offer in Mucina, Devi Dee. 2013. "Ubuntu Orality as a Living Philosophy." *The Journal of Pan African Studies, Volume 6, Number 4, 18 – 35.*

[2] This quote is drawn from p. 108 in the work of Wane, N. N. (2000). Reflections on Mutuality of Mothering: Women, Children and Othermothering. Association of Research in Mothering Journal, 2(2), 105-116 (A-12).
the work

Embers of
Micro-aggression

DIBIKGEEZHIGOKWE

T ODAY WAS THE FIRST DAY in a very long time that I felt genuinely happy. So long that I surprised myself with the heart-warming laughter, smiles, and fun I had with my son and my partner. It felt as though I had been in a deep slumber and finally awoke.

Then I read your email.

You know, that same fucking one you send to me when you feel attacked by my mere presence. The one where you think for certain that you are asserting your boundaries with me – your white feminist, borderland.

Within the first five seconds, I feel the now familiar anger I have toward you. My anger at one time looked like a raging fire. But, after four painstaking years with you, it has become the hot, red embers of a long lasting, tendered, and nurtured fire. My embers burn strong within the next two minutes after reading your email.

When my son and partner talk to me now, five minutes after I read your email, I am no longer the happy Momma, and lighthearted partner. I embody my embers, and sizzle and crackle when they talk to me. I distance myself, come into myself, and wallow in my contempt for you.

The hour passes.

This is when my immense exhaustion sets in. Well, hello, my old familiar companion. I've had not even one day to enjoy your absence. I had only the morning and afternoon to delight in my rare happiness

until

I decided to open the white, feminist's email.

From a Place of Love

ERYNNE M. GILPIN

if you are softer
than before
they came.
you
have been loved.

-nayyirah waheed

COLONIALISM IS ALIVE AND WELL. Embedded within a politics of fear, racism and fossil fuel, colonial values situate the individual as an isolated figure within a hierarchy of power, privilege, and competition. The insidious effects of colonialism imprint themselves within a social psyche and colonialism itself is predicated on the erasure of Indigenous worldview and emergent Nationhoods. Perhaps it is useful to move beyond attempts to define colonialism and rather explore ideas which help us understand how colonialism defines us.

In the face of violent dispossession, explosive development and significant disruption of *being Indigenous*, many of us experience a profound rage against colonial projects in this work. It is not uncommon for us to witness or even channel this rage into our own relationships.

For many of us, colonial enterprise violently dispossesses Indigenous families and communities from our cultural birth-rites, governance protocols, languages and ceremonial life. Many of us are left picking up the pieces, and simultaneous are required to critically interrogate ongoing colonial projects as well as contribute to authentic efforts towards our own community's cultural and political resurgence. This is not to discredit the power and possibilities of politics of our rightful rage, but to extend the conversation towards possibilities of other political emergencies of experience and emotion.

Indigenous love is alive and well. Love for our people. Love for the Lands and Waters that raised us, and love for emergent political imaginaries, beyond colonialism. In this way, *Everyday Acts of Resurgence* is a project of decolonial love. I consider the possibility of love, as a viable political mechanism within the larger movements towards Indigenous sovereignty, resurgence and regeneration. Can love, as connection, be a tangible tool for dismantling colonial violence inside of our own hearts and in the world around us? Finally, how can the notion of decolonial or Indigenized love speak to emerging global Indigenous nationalist consciousness?

While conversations about love often do not make their way into the political arena, I am interested in how the potential of decolonial love can guide our discussions and actions of resurgence and decolonization. Love teaches us to not only acknowledge interconnected relationships, but also how to enact a practice of accountability and respect to these relations.

Love is softness and patience with the other. Love demands truth and freedom from fear, but must first come from a place within and to ourselves. In this way, decolonial love is the enactment of conscious relationships to self, others, spirit and the Land and furthermore accountability to these relationships through patience, reciprocity and respect.

We know that this process must first come from the land.

Kitaskînaw î pî kiskinohamâkoya. Sâkihito-maskihkiy î pî Kiskinohamâkoya.

Our knowledge as a people (who relate to one another) comes from the land. How we relate to the land, determines how we relate to one another. We know that our genealogy extends into the Land and in turn extends into one another.

The land gives us our knowledge. The land gives us our Love. Noelani

Goodyear-Kaʻōpua advocates *"schools and educational systems that encourage our young people to fall in love with Āina (the land)".* Similarly, in her piece entitled *I am not a Nation State*, Leanne Simpson describes her deep wishes to have her "great grandchildren to be able to fall in love with every piece of our territory". Falling in love is a beautiful and creative journey. For anyone who has ever fallen in love knows that it requires patience, effort, time, honour and sometimes sacrifice. Both Goodyear- Kaʻōpua and Simpson describe how love is born a creative force which inspires creativity, abundance, and promotes life itself.

Many of our songs, poems and stories proclaim the love and rapture we have for the land. Engaging with her as kã wee coma aski, Original Mother, we recognize her as the embodiment of abundance. Revitalizing air, invigorating fires, soothing waters and rich earth surround us with plentitude. In constant giving, the earth gives life and abundance as love. The blueprints for peace technologies are encoded in individual strands of grass, and stories which provide purpose and meaning for our lives imprinted on mountain faces. Everything we need to live a good life is in and from the earth.

The renewal of our understanding of **love as action** is necessary in the integrity of our efforts towards regenerative Indigenous resurgence. To practice love as a daily commitment available to us in every single moment, and one place we each can manifest this practice is in our immediate relationships of our family; or those we belong to/with. To love is to situate ourselves as Indigenous people from a place of strength, creativity and wisdom.

To Love.

For myself, one of the biggest challenges in my own decolonial unbecoming is to step away from the emphasis of I as individual or separate from another. It takes an incredible amount of effort to set aside the individual ego, pride and self-righteousness and embody values of our ancestors. Values which challenge us to position ourselves in wisdom, good-humour and realness.

When it is hard for me to be fully accountable for my own actions and privileges, I am required to take the time and effort to understand my own discomfort or challenges and allow it into my life. Perhaps when we reflect from a place of love, we can engage in meaningful discussions which focus on self-work and accountability rather than pointing out the flaws or imperfections of another. If we are able to move beyond these feelings of discord, perhaps we can experience a softening to first ourselves, and then eventually towards others. How interesting it would be if our collective conversations about accountability required us to first and foremost identify our own particular responsibilities and commitments to one another. How beautiful it would be to ask one another not how we define love, but rather how love defines us?

This will look different for each one of us, and we are accountable to ourselves to discern what self-love looks like. Just as the land embodies abundance, we are asked to be abundant in the way in which we relate to the world around us. This is an act of great courage. A commitment to truth. A quiet, intimate and everyday act of resurgence.

The prayer below is one sent to me from my Great Uncle Ted.

It asks the Creator for the courage to live in truth, seek wisdom and be of one mind.

Kisemanito. li kourawch miyinawn. Paray chee itayhtamawk. Kwayesh kapiouhtayhk. Marsee chee itwayak ka kishcheetayimoyak. Nitataminan.

Ayis kiyehewini Pimatisiwin. Sayweyiminan mena ota mamawai kayayahk. Meyinan, muskawisewin mena ayimesewin. Ta natohtamahk menata nehehtamahk. Meyinan asumena ta wapahatamahk Sakastiwewini mena ka nanskomitinanan. Hiy Hiy anaskomitinanan

places

Changes in the Land,
Changes in Us

TAIAIAKE ALFRED

Y OU GO OUT ONTO THE LITTLE DOCK your grandfather built out of logs and tied down in the spring as soon as the water was warm so you could swim and fish off of it all summer long. Dipping the pail into the river you get some of the water your Doda will cook with. "Go get me some water for cooking and I'll make you something good to eat," she told you. Later when the sun starts to fade your Doda will be washing clothes in the river with a washboard and hanging them to dry in the trees. The water she cooks with is the same water you drink, and use to take a bath, the same water that you do everything in your lives with. You are alone and it is quiet now as you dip water in the early morning, but in the afternoon and at night there are people that come from the village to picnic or make fires and drink beer. Sometimes people leave their garbage, so you have to clean that up the next day. That's what you do, you and your grandmother, most days in the summer, after she makes you breakfast you start the day by cleaning up one of the beaches or your special fishing spot, picking up whatever is there messing up the shore or in the shallow water, making it nice again for families and the kids who live here to spend time on the shore and play in the water.

You always do it without complaining except for one time your Doda got fed up with some kids throwing their Kik Cola soda bottles on the ground and busting them on the rocks in the water, and she yelled at them to stop doing that and told them to pick up the broken glass. There was a family eating lunch at the flat rocks and the man got mad at her. He said something about the sharp words she used with those kids, even telling her she had a hard face for acting like she owned the beach. "This isn't your river, Konwakeri" he said, "you should just leave them kids alone." Your grandmother was always so soft-spoken, but utkon saraksen, you saw a different look in her eyes then, and she got mad at that man. But she didn't swear at him or anything like that. All she did was look right at his wife and say, "That's my house over there, and I've lived in it all my life. I know darn well I don't own the river or the land – nobody does. I don't need to be told that by you. But we are the ones who live here and who take care of this place, who clean it up every day and make it nice for people like you to come over here from town and use it." That's all she said, but she kept looking right at the wife. And the woman turned and looked at her husband, and that man just looked away and he didn't say anything else that whole day.

There is a rowboat tied to the dock and you look at it and think back to when she would take you out on the river, just you and her. You were still just small and sitting in the front of the boat while she was rowing up and down the shoreline, in the early morning, when it was so calm and quiet on the water. You hung your face over the side of the boat watching fish as it moved along slowly. You could see all the way to the bottom, and there were all kinds of fish in the water. Teionatienitare, a big sturgeon, swam right under your face and scared the heck out of you.

This one time she took you out onto the river towards one of the small islands and it clouded over and all of a sudden started to rain, and then a storm came up before you could make it back home. So she headed for the small island. When you got to the shore she turned the boat over and you sat with her under it in the rain and the wind. Your Doda held you tight and talked to you in a soft voice until the storm passed. When it did, she flipped the boat over and you kept on going to where you were headed. She took you out on the water in the summer and sometimes you'd have to stay under that boat for a long time, once even a whole night, just the two of you out there on a small island in the river. It was okay though because she always had something to eat with her and she always had lots of stories to tell.

Your grandfather uses the boat even more, when he's home from working away in New York. He asks her what kind of fish she wants to eat for supper and she tells him and he goes out and, every single time, a little while later, comes back with a bucket full of that kind of fish. He knows just where to go. The best day of your life was the time you went with him to gather some wood and do some fishing and you saw a big eel in the shallows near the shore. Somebody must have been spear fishing the night before and stabbed it, but it got away. It was hurt, but your Baba knew you were happy to have found it, and that it was just barely alive anyway so you didn't have to be afraid of it. Seeing that fish, he told you to go get a big long stick that's hook-shaped on the end, and you used that stick to drag that eel behind the boat all the way back to the dock. When you got back to dock and walked toward the house holding the eel, your Doda came out wiping her hands on her apron and with a big smile. "Whaaa, what a fisherman you are! The creator must have sent us this great fish so that we can eat good today," and she grabbed the eel with her hands, held it like it was a precious gift and thanked you for it. Then she turned around and threw it right into a pot of boiling water she had going on the stove. After a little while she pulled it out and the skin came off it so easy. She cut off all the meat and boiled it some more. That night she baked it and you all ate that eel for supper. Your Doda and Baba loved eating fish from the river, especially eels. They ate everything. Even you kids too, when you were by yourselves, you would get tin cans and bring them with you to the riverside and when you got hungry you would make little fires and boil some water. Then you would lift up rocks and find all kinds of crawfish, some as big as your hand. You would boil them up and eat them just like that right there. Not only fish, you used pick all kinds of plants and eat them too. There was this one, everybody called it tarakwi, and it was like a date, or a wild candy. You don't even know what they call it in English. Iowe:kon, everything was so good back then.

Your grandparents passed away a long time ago, and the small dock and their house are long gone. You are here living in the now, standing there by yourself on the shore where that little dock used to be, and you can't help but think about how life is so different today. When they moved everybody from the riverside to the village, it was like you became a race of people from somewhere else. They moved you away from the river and it didn't take long before you had trouble even imagining grandmas and little kids rowing boats against the current in the big river and grandfathers fishing for sturgeons, or young mothers crossing the train bridge over the river on foot and walking five miles to go to work, or people growing and hunting and trapping their own food. It was just a mile from the river to the place they moved your house to yet once you were away from the river and living in town it was like overnight everybody became city people, because then your lives were being lived turned away from the water, the Seaway was between you and the river, the place where you grew up and where the roots of your family went into the earth and where your father buried the cord that was cut when you were born. It is where your heart and true home are, still. Living in the village right on top of each other you didn't have the same feeling about your neighbors that you used to have when you lived on the riverside. Even the way you thought of your own family changed. People started keeping to themselves in their own little houses and they didn't help each other the way they did before.

For years you used to wonder why that was and how things got that way, but now you know. It's because on the riverside you didn't need money to be complete and to feel happy. They took away your land to build the Seaway and after that your connections to that place and the land got weak; the land was now just a street you lived on, a quarter acre of property that you put a fence around to make sure your neighbors didn't come onto it, where you built your new and better houses with insulated walls and indoor toilets. After you moved from the riverside you all had jobs and cars and TVs, but you couldn't go to the riverside anymore where your grandparents used to live. You couldn't go on the river and fish for sturgeon and eels, or float down the river on a log past the black bridge and then walk to the place along the shore where the bushes used to be so thick it was like going into a long, dark maze with the berry bushes totally covering the path and hanging overhead like a tunnel. You couldn't walk through the bushes and just reach up over your head and pick ripe ahtahwakaion, the small, soft, red berries shaped like thimbles and handfuls of strawberries too that were hanging down on the path, and there were no women and kids gathered there anymore eating their fill and loading up big black ash baskets with wild berries.

You can't do any of that now because it's all noxious weeds and gravel and concrete and junk metal strewn all over the dirt under the footings of the Mercier Bridge. You have money, but you don't have the land. You need money, and your need for money has changed everything, the land, the water, and it has changed you too.

When they came to build the Seaway, they made your Doda pack all her stuff and move and they bull-dozed her house while she stood there watching with tears flowing from her eyes. They made her move, but before she did she left her washboard right there on the shore. When she left the riverside for the last time she leaned her washboard up against her favorite tree, a nice big willow with huge braches and roots. That was her last stand, and it was the mark she wanted to leave. It used to be right there, on a spot you can't even go to now because it is right in the middle of the big channel they dug to make the Seaway. They chopped that tree down when they started work, and it's gone now too. You can still picture her standing there in the doorway of her house looking out over the point and the river that one last time. Was she sad to be leaving that place and that way of life or was she looking forward to leaving it all behind? From where you are standing, on what little land is left of the place your family lived for many generations, this tranquil bastion of the natural world and ancestral spirit, you feel her heart breaking for the loss. The land is still there, the river is still flowing, but where are the people now? You turn and look the other way, over the Seaway at the government buildings, the houses, and roads and cars of the reserve on the other side, and you try hard to not see it as a far away land where foreign people are speaking a language that you can't understand.

Recovering Place Names from Hawaiian Literatures

NOENOE K. SILVA

INDIGENOUS RESURGENCE INCLUDES STRENGTHENING OUR TIES to ancestral places and languages. Reclaiming our native languages is key to the process of recovery. Settler colonialism in Hawai'i, as in many other places, attempts constantly to erase and replace native landscapes with a settler-built landscape. These forms of erasure include replacing native place names and/ or stripping native place names of their meanings through forceful assimilation tactics such as shifting the language to the colonial one. Kanaka 'Ōiwi Hawai'i are fortunate that our recent ancestors (since the 1820s) took up writing in the native language —'ōlelo Hawai'i —seriously and prolifically. The shift to English has made it arduous for current generations to learn our own native language at levels sufficient to understand the writing of our ancestors. We are, however, determined to do so, and thousands of us are doing so. In the literature written in 'ōlelo Hawai'i between the 1820s and the 1940s are thousands of place names. This essay explores the project of recovering Hawaiian place names from this treasure trove of literature.

Many recent Kanaka scholars have articulated the importance of our native place names. Kekuewa Kikiloi writes: "Place names are important cultural signatures etched into the Hawaiian landscape and are embedded with traditional histories and stories that document how our ancestors felt about a particular area . . . They help to transform once-empty geographic spaces into cultural places enriched with meaning and significance."[1] Kikiloi says that the names are etched into the landscape, but not all of those etchings are still visible and audible to us. Composer and eminent interpreter of Hawaiian texts Kīhei de Silva explains:

We live in a time of un-naming, in a time when old names for the land—
names given in honor, happiness, and sorrow—have been set aside for
marketing jingles that commemorate little more than a desire for sales
. . . We who learn and love these old names . . . seek nourishment in that
other deeper geography. [2]

In other words, settler colonialism writes over ancestral place names. This un-naming and renaming goes on as Hawaiian places are renamed and transformed for housing developments and resorts. One example is the area previously known as Kalāhuipua'a, an ahupua'a and fishpond in Kohala on Hawai'i Island. This place name appeared prominently on a sign until sometime in the early 1990s, when it disappeared and was replaced with signs for Mauna Lani resort. The name Kalāhuipua'a is translated by Pukui et al. as "family of pigs," which, it seems, the developers did not think a suitable name for the area of their resort. Mauna Lani (heavenly mountain) lies on the flat and rocky shoreline of Kalāhuipua'a. That resort has now incorporated Kalāhuipua'a into what they sell, calling it "the essence and spiritual center of the resort,"[3] but the mountain-less area's name is still Mauna Lani.

This example shows how place names get perpetuated, but in forms different from the original. In 'Ōiwi times, islands were divided into large districts called moku; within each moku were several to many ahupua'a; and within ahupua'a were smaller land divisions. Management of these large to small divisions was highly organized, as was the management of the freshwater flows and shoreline fishponds. Kalāhuipua'a was an ahupua'a, but its name is preserved only as the fishpond. In other cases, ahupua'a and smaller division names now appear as names of streets, for example, or neighborhoods. Most people are unaware of the origin of these street and neighborhood names.

In addition, we Kānaka are constantly perturbed by their mispronunciation, but perhaps also secretly pleased at the trouble they cause the settlers and visitors who have to try to pronounce them. For settlers, learning to pronounce these correctly would be one step towards their part in native resurgence, which Taiaiake Alfred describes as "to acknowledge our existence and the integrity of our connection to the land."[4]

Because of the work of Mary Kawena Pukui and others, we have a few reference works that give us the origins and meanings of some place names, but the majority remains unrecorded in reference books.[5] In *Place Names of Hawaii*, Samuel Elbert writes that the book includes 4,000 names. He also explains: "Even a rough estimate [of the number of Hawaiian place names] is impossible . . . Hawaiians named taro patches, rocks and trees that represented deities and ancestors, sites of houses and *heiau* . . . and the tiniest spots . . ."[6] Despite his apparent exasperation with the immensity of any project to record all the names, he contributed a great deal to our ability to do so and apparently also understood our need to have our 'āina carry the names our ancestors gave them.

Thus, while we have a lot of native place names, we have forgotten a lot of them because of the shift to English. I have been reading Hawaiian language literature of different genres for many years now, and a few years ago, I began to collect names that I couldn't find in our regular reference sources. The great majority of this literature was originally published in serial form in Hawaiian language newspapers, which for a long time were only partially and poorly indexed, and available mainly on microfilm. Today the majority have been scanned and are available online, and the project of making them searchable is proceeding now. The digitization of place names is something rarely thought of as part of a community resurgence process but it is an unacknowledged and important aspect of reclamation.

The value in gathering the names from mo'olelo, as opposed to maps or city directories, is that stories associated with the names are written there, too. Sometimes the stories tell us the origin of the names, and often, the names tell us characteristics of the place. They usually tell us something that happened at each place. One example is a place in the moku of Waialua here on O'ahu that was called Kamani or Ke Kamani a Hamanalau; the woman Hamanalau brought seeds of a kamani tree from Molokai and planted a grove for which the place was named.

Many moʻolelo are overflowing with names of places. Sometimes these are remembered in lists that can function as mnemonics for place names and their winds or rains, and also as maps. For example, in the moʻolelo of the volcano deity Pele, she calls the names of winds in order to literally blow away her rivals for the affections of her lover. Those rivals also happen to be moʻo (reptilian water deities) dangerous to humans. According to my research assistant Hoʻoleia Kaʻeo, Pele calls the names of 273 winds of 198 different place names from the islands of Nihoa, Lehua, Kaʻula, Niʻihau, and Kauaʻi. In addition to this list, Kaʻeo collected all of the place names from this moʻolelo written by Joseph Mokuʻōhai Poepoe and published between 1908 and 1911, many of which are not found in the reference sources. Her method was to go through a print copy of the moʻolelo page by page, identify the place names, and then check the current reference sources.

For another project, I read many works written by an author named Joseph Kānepuʻu. I collected 43 place names from his works that are not in our sources. Other scholars are making it a bit easier to do this. For example, Collette Leimomi Akana transcribed, annotated, and translated a portion of the moʻolelo of Kamapuaʻa from 1891, and her notes indicate which place names were not found in the reference sources.[7] Other works of transcription or retyping with contemporary orthography include lists of the place names in the moʻolelo, such as Hoʻoulumāhiehie's version of the Pele and Hiʻiaka moʻolelo published by Puakea Nogelmeier.[8]

Our information is scattered over different kinds of books right now, and some of the formats are outdated, such as the indispensable *Place Names of Hawaii.* In that book, each island was divided into quadrants and then each place name entry gives the quadrant. I want to be able to make this information accessible in ways that are most useful for both other scholars and the general public. Today, many of us are more interested in and able to identify places by moku and ahupuaʻa so that they can become part of our everyday actions again.

I close by recognizing that I am just one of many Kānaka working on renaming our ʻāina aloha (beloved lands) with their ancestral names. These are acts of resurgence only when many of us are engaged in them. E ola mau ka ʻōlelo kumu o ka ʻāina aloha.

NOTES

[1] Kekuewa Kikiloi, "Rebirth of an Archipelago: Sustaining a Hawaiian Cultural Identity for People and Homeland," Hūlili: Multidisciplinary Research on Hawaiian Well-Being 6 (2010): 75.

[2] Kīhei de Silva, "Liner Notes for 'O Ka'ōhao Ku'u 'āina Nani" (unknown, 1993).

[3] http://www.maunalani.com/press/fact-sheet-kalahuipuaa-at-mauna-lani Accessed February 3, 2017.

[4] Alfred, *Wasáse*, 19.

[5] Mary Kawena Pukui, Samuel H. Elbert, and Esther T. Mookini, *Place Names of Hawaii*, Rev. and enl. ed (Honolulu: University Press of Hawaii, 1974); John R. K. Clark, *Hawai'i Place Names: Shores, Beaches, and Surf Sites* (Honolulu: University of Hawai'i Press, 2002); Lloyd J. Soehren, Hawaiian Place Names, http://ulukau.org/cgi-bin/hpn?e=&a=q. Accessed February 3, 2017.

[6] Mary Kawena Pukui, Samuel H. Elbert, and Esther T. Mookini, *Place Names of Hawaii*, Rev. and enl. ed. (Honolulu: University of Hawai'i Press, 1976), ix–x.

[7] Collette L. Akana-Gooch, trans., *The O'ahu Exploits of Kamapua'a, the Hawaiian Pig-God: An Annotated Translation of a Hawaiian Epic from* Ka Leo O Ka Lahui, *July 23, 1891-August 26, 1891* (Honolulu: Bishop Museum Press, 2004).

[8] Ho'oulumāhiehie, *Ka Mo'olelo O Hi'iakaikapoliopele: Ka Wahine I Ka Hikina a Ka Lā, Ka U'i Palekoki Uila O Halema'uma'u - The Epic Tale of Hi'iakaikapoliopele: Woman of the Sunrise, Lightning-Skirted Beauty of Halema'uma'u*, trans. Puakea Nogelmeier (Honolulu, Hawai'i: Awaiaulu Press, 2006).

Mālama ʻĀina Koholālele

Recalling the Roots of our Resurgence

NOʻEAU PERALTO

ON A BALMY SATURDAY MORNING in November 2013, I gathered with other members of Hui Mālama i ke Ala ʻŪlili near a popular local fishing spot that most people refer to today as "Paʻauilo Landing," or just "the Landing." It was our first day of work on a community garden project we had envisioned years prior. The idea to start a garden down near the Landing emerged out of several experiences and conversations we had shared that had moved us towards re-establishing an ʻohana-centered space to return our hands to the land, and to share the food and stories of this ʻāina with others in our community. Over the years, this century and a half old government ship landing had become overgrown with invasive weeds and littered with the waste of a careless few. With nothing more than the tools in our hands and the aloha in our na'au, our hui worked together that morning to clear the 'āina of invasive guinea grass, remove truck loads of trash, and plant a few of our native food plants. We are not the owners or the lessees of this 'āina. We have no codified "rights" to it other than the kuleana embodied in our bones. We are simply the 'Ōiwi descendants of this 'āina, following the instructions of those who came before us: if you mālama this 'āina, it will mālama you.

When we took a break for lunch, I recall our kupunawahine, Aunty Millie Bailado saying, "We need to give this māla (garden) a name." Naming imbues mana, spiritual power. "How about Mālama 'Āina Koholālele?" she suggested. We all agreed on the name, which was immediately painted on a small sign and placed in the middle of the māla. Such a simple name would not pique the attention of many. "Mālama 'Āina Koholālele"—Caring for the 'Āina of Koholālele. It's pretty straight forward. But considering that this 'āina has been exploited as "property" for over a century and called by the name of the sugar plantation mill it serviced for just as long, an act as "everyday" as consciously calling a place by its proper ancestral name is profound. This everyday act of resurgence not only counters the erasure of the name, histories, and genealogies of Koholālele, it further reasserts our responsibilities as the descendants of this place to mālama 'āina—to care for and protect the long-term well-being of that which sustains us physically and spiritually as a people.

In the days of our kūpuna, not many generations ago, the ahupua'a of Koholālele was dedicated by the ruling chiefs of this island as a pu'uhonua, a sacred place of refuge and healing. The cliffs of Koholālele were famous, known in mo'olelo as a place where the akua sisters of Maunakea—Poliahu, Lilinoe, and Kalauakolea—would frequent, waiting to entice unsuspecting passerbys to ascend the mountain with them. These high cliffs were also celebrated in mele, songs and chants, as favored places for Hāmākua's skilled and courageous fishermen to descend to the sea by rope, to fish or gather 'opihi. In Koholālele our kūpuna constructed a heiau named Manini, which functioned as a kū'ula and was dedicated to the practice of ho'oulu 'ai, the growth of food. The ritual practice of ho'oulu 'ai ceremonies at Manini ensured the abundance of food resources in the sea and on the land in Hāmākua. It was this understanding of the spiritual foundations of aloha 'āina and mālama 'āina rooted in place that enabled and empowered our kūpuna to cultivate these 'āina in ways that were not only extremely productive, but more importantly, pono. Every person who has eaten of the bounty of this ʻāina and its seas has been a beneficiary of these works of our kūpuna. Now the time has come for our generation to take on this kuleana to continue to hoʻoulu ʻai—regenerate the systems that sustain us.

When a child is born, it is customary for an elder in the family to gift the child with a name. In some instances, ancestral names are given to imbue the child with the desirable characteristics and mana of its original forbearer. The ancestral name that Aunty Millie gifted to the māla we gave birth to that day alludes to many of the reasons why our ancestors of Koholālele, "the breaching humpback whale," understood it to be so important. In the ocean, the koholā (humpback whale) migrates each year between the cold waters of the north and the warm waters of Hawaiʻi. Throughout this journey, the koholā releases sacks of mucus, called hūpē koholā, in which ʻōhua, baby fish, like that of the manini, live until they reach maturity. As these hūpē koholā float throughout the ocean, they act as seed banks, replenishing the sea with new generations of fish. In this way, the ʻāina of Koholālele also served the physical and spiritual function of ensuring the abundance of the ocean and its many resources. Koholālele, like the ocean dwelling ancestor for which it was named, is life-giving and sacred—from its most ma uka boundary at Puʻu o Kiha on the slopes of Maunakea, to the depths of its rugged seas—and it requires our care and protection.

For the majority of our people today, however, the name Koholālele exists solely in the footnotes of our history texts—texts that most of our youth will never be introduced to in the current public education system. Generations of plantation exploitation have reinscribed our landscape with names that were appropriated by sugar companies for their mills, relocation camps, and landings, like "Paʻauilo Landing." There are no road signs, street names, or stores that bear Koholālele's name today. Just the small, hand-painted sign in the middle of our māla. "Mālama ʻĀina Koholālele," says it all. We have not forgotten the names of our ancestors. We have not forgotten our responsibilities to care for them. The ʻŌiwi caretakers of this ʻāina are here to stay. We are pulling the weeds of our dependence, recalling the roots of our resurgence, and replanting the seeds of our reemergence as the thriving descendants that our ancestors prayed for. And it all began with some seemingly "everyday" actions. Gather with your family. Clear a space. Make a garden. Gift it a name. And commit to it.

As we gathered at the end of that first tranformative workday, one of our hui leaders and organizers, Aunty Loke Alpiche expressed, "A garden represents growth, and the seed was planted today." We cleared a space for growth together that day, planted "the seed," and since then, much growth has come from that garden. In just little over a year, our Mālama 'Āina Koholālele māla has doubled, tripled, and quadrupled in size. While at that first workday in 2013 just about 30 hands were (re)turned to the soil, over the past three years over 1500 hands have come together to mālama this 'āina. And not only have we grown in size and number. The cultivation of this garden and the fulfillment of our shared kuleana together has grown our relationships with this land and with each other. Laulima. Many hands working together grow stronger together. They learn from each other. Feed each other. Protect each other. Care for each other. Heal each other. Our kūpuna teach us to "huli ka lima i lalo," turn your hands down to the soil, "he ola ko laila," for that is where life emerges from.

Hands covered in 'āina and grasped firmly together, we stood in a circle together to offer a closing pule for the continued growth of our māla, breathing intention into our actions, telling the seeds we planted that day to bare fruits for as long as our descendants shall live on this 'āina. When our pule was complete, the eldest in our circle, Aunty Millie, offered her gratitude for the work we had all come together to complete, and reaffirmed her commitment to the presence we had rebirthed in Koholālele that day. "Our garden here is small. I like it very much, and am happy here. This place is special, and I will always be here. No matter what, I will always be here." The roots of our resurgence run deep in this 'āina. And it is in our everyday actions to ensure that these roots "will always be here" that we renew our relationships and responsibilities to the source from which our well-being as a people emerges. E mau ke ea o ka 'āina.

Represencing Indigenous peoples in the landscape

the Spirit of Quandamooka

LISA STRELEIN[1]

EMPLACEMENT, and the intimate and enduring relationship between people and place, is essential to Indigenous traditions of thought and ways of being in the world. In Australia as well as throughout the world, the relationship between Indigenous peoples and Country is a foundational aspect of law, cultural practice, ceremony and history, as well as philosophical and epistemological concepts expressed through language and place. Disconnection from land, then, through dispossession or impairment of enjoyment is more than merely a transfer of property or economic deprivation.

As a non-Indigenous person trained in the western traditions of legal and political thought, I often think and write about the duality of measures of 'justice' as at once colonising and decolonising – as both empowering and disempowering; and of the failure of imagination in adapting western traditions to better understand our relationship with place in order to respectfully engage with Indigenous peoples on more than a legal and economic plane.[2]

When I think about the cost and what is gained by land claims and settlement processes, it is easy to question the validity of my own contribution to making these systems work. But then, I reflect back to the driving force that spurs communities to assert their right and responsibility to speak for Country. And I look to the genuine pride and relief that is so often expressed by those who successfully navigate the difficult legal and political battles that accompany the assertion of rights of Country.

My friend and colleague, Quandamooka leader and historian Dr Valerie Cooms has spoken of the strength of the Quandamooka spirit, which has been invigorated and reinforced as a direct consequence of the successful native title claim over their traditional Island home, Minjerribah, which we also know as North Stradbroke Island.

Quandamooka Country extends beyond Minjerrabah itself, and comprises the waters and lands of Moorgumpin (Moreton Island), the Southern Moreton Bay and Stradbroke Islands. It includes the mainland from the mouth of the Brisbane River to the Logan River on the coast of what is now known as south-east Queensland.

Since very early in Queensland's colonial history North Stradbroke Island has been a playground for Brisbane holidaymakers who take advantage of the world-renowned north facing white sand surf beaches. The arrival by ferry in the middle of the local Quandamooka community and perhaps without ever knowing it, the visitors head to the exclusive beachfront settlements. They are ignorant of the blood of the dolphin spirit that washes the rocks of the shore next to the ferry terminal; they do not acknowledge the ancestors whose spirits live in the trees surrounding them or the spiritual significance of the sand and sea. And they do not acknowledge the Quandamooka people on whose land they have established their occasional homes.

Asserting rights to Quandamooka country through the native title system was costly, both in financial terms and in the trauma that the application

Quandamooka Country

process creates for the community. So why go through it? For many Indigenous peoples there is no choice but to take the courses of action that best enable them to give some measure of protection to their traditional country and to achieve the recognition and survival of their people.

I recently had the opportunity to visit Valerie on her Country and the visibility of the Quandamooka people on the Island was palpable. Unmistakable signs declared these lands as Quandamooka Aboriginal land and the branding of the traditional owner corporation 'the Spirit of Quandamooka' was everywhere.

This visibility is deliberate and meaningful, as Valerie explains:

> I expect to see children growing up with the expectation that native title is there. My granddaughter ... was born into knowing that this is our [native title organisation]. ...She'll be able to drive around Stradbroke Island as a young child and see this is Quandamooka Aboriginal land, a sign that was never there. My mother never got to see it, my grandfather didn't get to see it, my older brother didn't get to see it but I did and my grandkids will and my children will. There are big green signs on the island and it doesn't matter how many times you drive past it, every time you see it you realise, and then the tourists will see it and the visitors will see it and that's our brand. That's always good to see.

As family Elder and Chair of the native title organisation, Valerie, more than most, confronts the recalcitrance and colonising imperative of governments in the continued breaches of agreements and resistance to change. But now the Quandamooka people engage in this relationship from a position of greater influence. Visitors are now *yura*, welcome.

Importantly, the Quandamooka people have the breathing space to turn their energy away from those conflictual engagements and instead expend and gain energy from positive engagement with Country.

The native title settlement has given the Quandamooka Elders the opportunity to provide every young Quandamooka person the opportunity (and concomitant responsibility) to work on Country and represent the Spirit of Quandamooka. The Elders have also had an opportunity to re-frame the 'atlas' of the Island, ascribing the cultural values that need to be taken into account in land use planning and development decisions.

The 're-presencing' of Indigenous peoples in their territories (that is, both physical and philosophical reoccupation) has provided a more effective remedy to dispossession and colonisation than perhaps could have been predicted.

Re-presencing in this sense is not just place names (although all cultures know that there is power in the true names of places), it is about changing the way the landscape is understood, its about how, and by whom, decisions are made about access and use of lands, about how 'sustainable development' is defined and to whom benefits accrue. It extends to what is taught in schools on country, what history is told and what laws are respected.

In the end re-presencing is about how the people stand in the land and feel in their skin, everyday. For Indigenous peoples, this is knowing that responsibilities have been met and relationships to Country are restored. For non-Indigenous peoples it may well be a level of discomfort and reorientation, both in their relationship with the ecosystems that they inhabit, and to the authority of Indigenous voices speaking for Country.

It will be some time before the community of Stradbroke Island and the Queensland Government adjusts to the Quandamooka people being the largest landowners on the Island, the largest commercial operation as well as equal partners in environmental management. Too often agreements are reached only to confront the response – 'but we didn't know that we would be expected to change the way we do things'!

For many colonising peoples, there is a genuine desire to find a sense of justice and legitimacy in our relationships with Indigenous peoples but there is an abject failure to adjust our habits of thought about relationships to Country. Legal rights and economic settlements, however imperfect, provide a layer of protection against the impetus to colonise that is innate in our institutions and ideologies.

My interest and responsibility is to be vigilant and aware of the need to maximise the capability of my own institutions of law and politics to be decolonising and empowering, wherever possible. There is potential in these moments to create space for Indigenous peoples to breathe and to reconnect without the assault of colonising institutions and forces – to be free to choose and to develop in ways that retain the connection to land and the obligations of law, to engage in everyday acts of cultural resurgence and enliven the spirit.

NOTES

[1] This paper as authored in consultation with Dr Valerie Cooms, Quandamooka Elder and Chair of the Quandamooka Yoolooburrabee Aboriginal Corporation (QYAC). I would like to express my thanks to Val and to QYAC for sharing their story and important cultural information with me and allowing me to share it more broadly.

[2] See, for example, Strelein, L and Tran T, 2013 'Building Indigenous Governance from Native Title: Moving away from 'Fitting in' to Creating a Decolonised Space' 18(1) Review of Constitutional Studies 19-47.

Fearless
Regeneration

Walking with
Decolonial Intention
on Indigenous Land

SENKA ERIKSEN

I N TODAY'S URBAN CENTERS most people rely on cars to get them around. Being fast matters. I don't blame them. It is convenient and arguably necessary in some cases. When I tell people I don't drive they are often surprised and confused. I have driven cars and I do know how, but I choose not to. I walk. I choose to walk because it allows me to access the movements of my body. I move with the land under my feet and the air passing over my skin into my body as I breathe. Moreover, I walk slowly. I have Arthritis, and the pain reminds me to slow down. This struggle has gifted me with gratitude. I can move my body. In these moments of struggle, I slow down and I'm brought more deeply into the moment, into my body. I can see and feel where I am. I see and feel the lands I walk on. Thus, walking has become an intentional act of decolonization and resurgence for me. It is a deeply embodied way of moving myself from one place to another. There is a contemplative aspect that is conducive to a deeper reflexivity. It is through this deeper reflexivity that my body and mind can intentionally engage in transformative imagination.

I grew up in the woods of the Semihamoo First Nation Rez and along the ocean shores of the Semiahmoo Bay. At low tide, the Semiahmoo Bay retreats at least a kilometer out, leaving behind an endless stretch of grey, undulating sand dotted with glistening tide pools full of sea grass and teaming with life. On the shore, there are often great rolls of decomposing brown, green and ochre seaweed. My first memories of walking are intimately connected to these coastal lands and waters. As such, I feel a deep and embodied relationship to them. While this relationship is valid in terms of intimacy, it is distinctly and often deliberately misrepresented in terms of legitimacy. Although settlers are an extant part of the lands they occupy, they have a different relationship with Indigenous land and it is my contention that settlers need to see this difference as sacred.

The settler location is shaped by the choices and actions of our ancestors, those who came before us, as well as by our contemporary engagements. By acknowledging this and walking with decolonial intention, we can begin to experience places in a different way. We begin to deconstruct colonial oppression by starting with the settler self in relation to Indigenous land. Part of deconstructing colonial oppression means recognizing contemporary markers of settler colonialism. This is primarily evident through state regulation/ exploitation of land, ideologies of entitlement and the Western normalization of our everyday lives; how we birth, eat, sleep, bath, live, love, make love, raise families and how we die. By reflecting on and confronting the positionality of these ideologies and normalizations, settlers can become fearless regenerators of relationships and create a strong foundation not only for equitable nation to nation relations, but also for a new way of being for settlers. And in order to actualize a new way of being, settlers must do the work that needs to be done in terms acknowledging and becoming accountable for the continuation of inequity, racism, entitlement and privilege.

So how can I decolonize and align myself with Indigenous nationhood? In terms of decolonial intention, I can try and open my eyes to what is around me in this place at this time. I can confront colonial systems, lobby for change, act with agency and refuse to remain silent in the face of racism, discrimination and oppression. I can speak my truths. I can pull up invasive plant species under the guidance of local Indigenous peoples and in doing so I can pull out some of the colonial roots Western culture has embedded within me. I can offer my skills, be available for community when invited, support grassroots initiatives and stand alongside Indigenous land protectors. I can work in community gardens and learn to listen to the water, the dirt and the plants. I can unlearn and relearn and align myself with Indigenous communities and people and with allied non-indigenous communities to find better ways in which to coexist. I can live my life in ways that reconnect, regenerate and reimagine a way of being that nurtures the land, the water and living beings and that promotes self-determined Indigenous nationhood.

Through these acts, I can begin to see that settler colonial reality is a permeable manifestation that primarily exists because it is enacted upon by many bodies willing to accept this reality as status quo. Its entire existence is wholly based on the imaginations of people immersed within capitalistic imperialism and shape shifting colonial confabulations. One senses that there is another reality that exists alongside of the settler colonial manifestation. An emergent reality based on deeper relationships between the land and human beings. The land seems to call out for resurgence. I think about this and what that means for the visitor, the trespasser, the immigrant and the settler. I wonder what this place would look like if power balances were restored. How would this place be expressed on the land and between communities? Would it be possible for nonindigenous people to relearn ways of moving our bodies and interacting with each other's bodies with authentic and responsible accountability? What would this look like?

In March, 2015 our IGOV cohort visited the Ho`oulu `Aina in the Kokua Kalihi Valley, Hawai'i. As we walked down a long dirt path, surrounded by tropical forest, we were greeted by sign which stated, "This land is your grandmother and she loves you". I never really thought of land as my grandmother. Nor have I thought of my grandmother as part of this land. I realized that although her bones are buried within Semiahmoo Territory and not in her own homelands of Lønstrup, Denmark, the land still deeply loves her. Part of changing the settler colonial reality is changing settler's stories of themselves, where we came from, why we came here and how we build relationships with the Original Peoples of the lands we live on. Part of this relationship includes re-storying settler colonial narratives and assertions of what reality is and finding our own truths which align us with Indigenous nationhood. This means understanding that the decisions of our ancestors are now our responsibility. This is how we settlers can begin to cultivate a legitimate relationship with this land.

In her article, *Ke Ku'e Kupa'a l oa Nei Makou—We Most Solemnly Protest: A Memoir of 1998*, Noenoe Silva (Kanaka Maoli) tells us that our ancestor's struggles are our struggles. Our ancestors walk alongside of us. I cited this to a friend the other day and they said that if we do not listen to our ancestors they will eventually close the door to walking with us. I thought about what that means in terms of settlers and our refusal to acknowledge that our ancestors actions are our responsibility. Are we so far removed from our ancestors that the door has been closed? Perhaps we have to reimagine what that door looks like. Reimagine a door that is shaped in the right way and leads us to a new way of being that is not colonial, imperial, capitalistic, benevolent, racist, sexist, heteronormative, ableist, neoliberal, and patriarchal with all the social suffering and harm that comes with these concepts. Instead, let it be abounding with expressions of decolonial intention. Let our walk together be filled with struggle, hard work, resurgence, healing and let it be overflowing with deep embodied love.

Walking in Hawaii

My being is full
My eyes are full with green plants, blue skies, smiling faces
And tears of gratitude
My nose is full with kalo fields, fragrant herbs, salt air
And the embrace of flowers
My ears are full with song birds, melodic chanting, loud winds
And children laughing
My tongue is full with good food, cool water, new words
And ancestors stories
My skin is full with warm sun, ocean water, bursts of rain
And many kisses
My mind is full with disconnections, reconnections, contrasts
And convergences
My heart is full with many answers, more questions, ongoing struggles,
And unlimited beauty
My being is full

Dän k'í[1]

SHELBY BLACKJACK

I see no false representation here

I am not the great white saviour

Or the prophesied red leader

I am always me

A daughter

A sister

A niece

An aunty

A cousin

Egay[2]

Eyénjyál[3]

I see no false representation here

I stand as a visitor to these lands

This stolen Hawai'i nui a kea[4]

A guest on this island

This piko[5]

This water

This wind

I see no false representation here

This is not my ea[6]

This is not my breath

That struggles for sovereignty on this land

But we can share this ea

This co-opted breath

This colonial mess we live in

This long ago warrior state

This north and this south

This sacred piko

I see no false representation here

I know what to do

To build strength

To build fire

To breathe

To rise up

I am always me

On my land

With my people

With my Dän k'í

Thoughts on
Dän k'í

I WROTE THIS POEM WHILE SITTING IN THE MIDST OF THE BEAUTY that is Oahu. I felt a pull to stay, to join in the fight to protect the land and the traditional way of life there, but I realised that it is not my piko to fight for. I can be an ally to the Kanaka Maoli from my home territory; I can respect and honor the warriors that I met there by fighting to protect my home territory as hard as they protect theirs. I believe that we are born into the nations that need us. We are their warriors, their voices, their protectors. Globally we unite to fight the larger battles, as allies, as sisters and as brothers.

NOTES
[1] Dän k'í – Indigenous way of being, in the Northern Tutchone Language
[2] Egay – A Wolf, in the Northern Tutchone Language
[3] Eyénjyál – A Woman, in the Northern Tutchone Language
[4] Hawai'i nui a kea – Kanaka Maoli original name of the Hawaiian Islands
[5] Piko – place in Kanaka Maoli
[6] Ea - to breathe, to rise up in Kanaka Maoli

practices

Dreaming is an Everyday Act of Resurgence

NOELANI GOODYEAR-KA'ŌPUA

U NFORTUNATELY, I grew up surrounded by American popular culture
that taught me to be afraid of ghosts. The ghosts on TV and in the movies
were not like people I knew. On my favorite cartoon show Scooby-Doo
and Shaggy were always running away from the ghoul who was out to get them.
The ghosts were named things like Ebenezer Crabbe, Mamba Wamba, or the
Headless Horseman. (There were no Ebenezers or Mambas in my second-grade
class, nor in my family.) And in the choose-your-own-adventure and horror-
stories-for-kids books that I loved to read between classes or on long car rides,

the supernatural was always frightening, associated with brutal murders, mysterious kidnappings, or tortured hauntings. Bloody knives. Prom dresses saturated with embalming fluid. Spirits out for revenge. It is no wonder that I was afraid of the dark and what night might bring.

Colonial violence aims to sever relationships. My own paralyzing fearfulness of ghosts and the alienation that caused between me and my ancestors is just one example of the violence that colonialism does to our spirits and, consequently, to our families and nations. Once my grandmother told me a story about her sister being pushed off the couch by a spirit during her nap. I automatically envisioned a harmful, belligerent ghost who was laying in wait until my aunty had fallen asleep. I could not imagine any other possibilities. Like, perhaps it was her deceased great-grandmother kicking her lazy butt off the couch to do the chores, tend to the family graves, or complete some other important task. Perhaps it was her younger sister who died a premature death but still wanted to play. Maybe she was giggling from behind the couch. These possibilities never even entered my mind because of the way my imagination had been saturated by pop cultural images of ghosts as dangerous and strange.

This fear of the supernatural gripped me so tightly as a child that one evening I was sitting with my grandmother and I asked her to promise me that when she died she would not show herself to me in spirit form. I told her it would scare me too much. She hugged me tight and agreed, "of course, my dear." Today, there is no request that I regret more in my life than this thing I asked of my grandmother. Just six or seven years old, I was too young to recognize the structural violence that was shaping my plea.

My grandmother has always honored my naïve request and has never appeared to me during my waking hours since her death. But, we never made any agreements about my dreams.

*   *   *

If Indigenous resurgence is enacted on an individual level, one warrior at a time, then dreaming can be one method of seeking personal healing and inspiration. For years after my grandmother's death, I had a recurring dream that I was running through the brightly-lit hallways of Kaiser Moanalua hospital, looking frantically for her room but never finding her in time to say goodbye. She had been quietly suffering from diabetes for years, never wanting to see a doctor. When we finally took her in, she needed to have one of her feet amputated. Just as we were making plans for how she would be able to get around our two-story town home, she took a turn for the worst. I was swimming laps at school when my high school PE teacher stopped me and dad rushed us over to the hospital. We didn't make it in time. And so, I had been searching for her, crying and running in my dreams for years afterward.

Finally she appeared. She was lying on one of the beds in our house, reassuring me that she was fine. My grandfather, the love of her life who died well before my birth, walked into the bedroom. He hugged me, just as she had a few moments earlier. Then he walked over to her, picked her up and carried her over the threshold. They passed through the doorway like a young couple entering their new home for the very first time together.

This dream helped me to heal years of heartache about not getting to say goodbye and not fully expressing how much I loved my grandmother before she passed into the next realm. She was always one to keep a promise. She could not come to me in my waking hours. So, she came to me instead when I was asleep, just like the many times she had massaged my limbs, or stroked my forehead until I drifted off, feeling safe and attended by her. From then on, I began to take my dreams more seriously, to pay attention to them. They gave me a way to begin reconnecting with ancestors from whom I had been estranged by colonial fears.

Schooling does not encourage us to write our dreams down, to take our dreams seriously, to share them with others, to talk about and interpret them. This is a form of colonial violence, a way of dismissing ancestral connection and Indigenous epistemologies. Dreaming is not just an off-loading of unnecessary information, the brain purging that which it does not need. Kanaka Maoli and many other Indigenous people have always known that dreaming is a valid way of knowing and communicating.

American-style English language teaches us to think about dreams in a simplistic and binary way: either good or bad, *dreams* or *nightmares*. In the Hawaiian language, the general word for a dream is *moe'uhane*. Moe refers to sleeping or lying down, and 'uhane can be translated as spirit. We also have specific words for all kinds of dreams: erotic, portending, recollected, and many more. Dreams are often sources for naming children. Our kūpuna Hawai'i taught that dreaming opens portals to different ways of being and perceiving, ways to which we do not have immediate access when we are awake. While the body rests, the spirit can travel. Dreams can be bridges for crossing from one island to another one across the archipelago. They can be ways to speak across generations.

If Indigenous resurgence is enacted on collective levels, in families and communities, then certain dreams might be shared and collectively interpreted. For many, many years now my people have been fighting the desecration of our highest mountain and elder sibling, Mauna a Wākea (popularly known as Mauna Kea), by the construction of a massive, industrial astronomy complex, which includes the proposed Thirty Meter Telescope (TMT). This fight escalated in October 2014 when international investors and dignitaries gathered on our sacred summit for a ground-breaking ceremony for the TMT. Several kānaka aloha ʻāina, people who are devoted in love for our land, blocked the roadway and disrupted the ground-breaking ceremony. Several performed their own Native ceremonies to reaffirm the sacredness of our mountain—the place where Papa, our earth mother, and Wākea, our sky father, touch.

Mauna a Wākea is a place where many Hawaiian families have buried the piko, or umbilical cords, of newly-born babies for countless generations. Similarly, the mountain itself is a piko for us a nation. Scholar of Hawaiian literature and orature, Kīhei de Silva, reminds us that Mauna Kea and the wonderous Lake Waiau near the summit are recognized by our ancestors as "ka piko o Wākea . . . ka hena o nā kuahiwi" (the connecting point to Wākea. . . the mountains' mons pubis), as "ka wai kapu a Lilinoe" (the sanctified water of goddess-ancestress Lilinoe), and as "ka piko lālāwai o nā manaʻo" (the fertile center of thought and desire). Additionally, the mountain is part of the 1.8 million acres of Hawaiian national lands that were illegally grabbed by the US when it began its ongoing occupation of my homeland and country in 1898.

When trucks ascended the mountain this spring, in the Hawaiian season of Kū (god of politics and war), more kānaka aloha ʻāina engaged in a blockade to stop them from beginning construction of the TMT. On 2 April 2015, 31 protectors of the mauna were arrested by police forces of the settler state—the State of Hawaiʻi and Hawaiʻi county governments. That night, while my body lay in bed on Oʻahu, I had a moeʻuhane that took me to an open plain. Wākea was stretched out in his great expanse. As I slept, I told myself: "I must remember this dream." I ran through the images over and over for the next few days, until I finally had a quiet moment to write it all down. With my 8-month-old son sleeping on my chest, I tapped a description out with the keys on my phone. What came flooding out was the following poem:

*

Pō
glistening black
wide night sky
earth beneath my feet
I'm captivated
head cocked back
eyes fixed above.

Silvery clouds rush across a passage
swiftly, silently on winds
high above
swirling and dancing across
from left to right with an urgent speed
at a point immediately overhead
they strike a pose
briefly hold a formation
a design
familiar
old yet new
I stare
trying to figure out
what
who.

A sudden purposeful jolt
s/he pulls back
gathering up form,
mass,
mana
materialized
stylized
sacred
carved lines, shapes
cloud like wood and

pō, the grooved spaces.

There is no mistaking
a dog
two-headed
barking, fearless
protector
Kū
standing, shaking, shaping
air and earth
Kiaʻi
fierce with booming voice
Mauna
larger than life
out of the deep darkness
and ready.

*

Feeling that this dream was not for me alone, I crowd-sourced interpretations of this moeʻuhane through Facebook and face-to-face conversations with friends and family. The dog's two-headedness puzzled me most. Dogs appear in many of our cultural stories and a few of our akua (gods) and kupua (demigods or heros) are known to take dog forms. But, to my knowledge, we do not have two-headed animals or beasts in our moʻolelo (histories and stories).

Many possible interpretations of this two-headedness came forward in my exchanges with friends and family. Perhaps it represents the masculine and feminine energies, powerful when joined together as a two-spirited being. Perhaps it represents two mountains. Both Mauna Kea and Haleakalā on the neighboring island of Maui are being threatened by massive telescope construction projects. Perhaps it represents the two-pronged approach of resistance to the desecration of Mauna Kea, one taking a legal route to challenge the project in settler state courts and the other taking a direct action approach by standing on the mountain and physically blocking the vehicles there to do destruction. Perhaps it represents the uprising of our nation as whole. In the past year we have seen two major groundswells of everyday Kānaka speaking up: first against settler state recognition and second against construction on the piko of our archipelago. When the US Department of Interior held hearings on multiple islands about a proposed rule-making process for US federal recognition, the vast majority of Kānaka who testified at every meeting firmly told the DOI panel: go back to Washington, thanks. We don't need your recognition. We want our independence. And now, as I write, Kānaka across the archipelago are spontaneously organizing expressions of aloha ʻāina and flooding social media with images and commentary using the hastags #TMTshutdown, #KuKiaiMauna, #ProtectMaunaKea and #WeAreMaunaKea.

The truth I have come to realize is that the dog's two-headedness is all of these things at once. It is also a reminder that we must cultivate two minds to receive the ʻike (knowledge, sight) of the pō (night) and the ʻike of the ao (day). We need to exercise and hone both of these heads, both of these minds, if we are to be fierce and effective protectors of our sacred places.

Just like our Mauna, our dreams are piko. Moeʻuhane are convergences, in which ancestors can bring messages or deliver new souls. Colors can be smelled. Skies can bleed. Arms can give us flight. Hawaiian language and education scholar, Maya Saffery, was the first person I heard talk and write about piko as points of convergence. A piko can be the generative connection of distinct elements: the umbilical cord, the genitals, a border, a summit.

As of this writing, I have not yet been able to get up to Mauna a Wākea to join the resurgence of my lāhui at the piko of our ea (life, sovereignty, breath, rising). I have participated in rallies, hearings and ceremonies on Oʻahu in support of the blockade, but I haven't been able to get on a plane to Hawaiʻi island. Yet, I have dreamt it. My body has not been to the Mauna in three years, but my ʻuhane has made the pilgrimage as the great protector spirit rises.

So, this is a call to dream. To meditate on your moeʻuhane. To write them. To share them when it feels right. To invite your loved ones to do the same. To consider the possibilities for collective interpretation. If, as Jeff Corntassel says, Indigenous resurgence in its everyday-ness is about remembering, restorying, reinterpreting, reconnecting to past and future generations, relating to one another to maintain continuity and wholeness as a people, then dreaming can be an everyday act of resurgence.

NOTES
[1] https://apps.ksbe.edu/kaiwakiloumoku/kaleinamanu/he-aloha-moku-o-keawe/maunakea_o_kalani. Accessed 16 April 2015.

Bring the 'Umeke of Poi to the Table

HOKULANI AIKAU

I OPENED THE LID OF THE POI BOWL and memories of my Tūtū washed over me[1]. Tūtū moved in with us when I was a teenager. Before that we only saw her every few years when she and Kūkū came to Utah to visit. They always brought poi with them and Tūtū expertly prepared it for us. She always stirred the poi until it was smooth; we never ate lumpy poi. Sometimes Tūtū prepared frozen poi, which is tricky because when it thaws it is very lumpy. But she had a technique for that too. She put the frozen poi in a bowl, placed the bowl over a pot of boiling water and slowly heated the poi gently stirring until it was smooth. She was so patient. She never rushed the process. My mom used the microwave oven to thaw the poi, but Tūtū always placed the frozen poi in a bowl over a pot of boiling water and slowly heated it until it was smooth. Watching her prepare smooth, silky poi taught me patience and that a task done well must be done thoroughly and completely. A perfectly prepared bowl of poi on the table was what love looked like. This past February when I got home from work and opened the poi bowl the smell of two-day old poi, the pungent sour yet sweet smell of the early stages of fermentation, carried me back to watching Tūtū prepare poi in our kitchen.

As a Hawaiian kid who grew up in Utah, poi was a luxury item. We only ate it when someone brought it from "back home." Poi was so rare I wanted to hoard it, stretch it with water so it would last longer. But my dad rarely kept the poi for just our family, there was always enough to share. Aunties and uncles would be invited to our kitchen to eat poi served with sardines, sweet onions, and tomatoes marinated in shoyu, vinegar and chili pepper water. Laughter and stories filled our home as the poi and mea 'ai (food) filled our 'ōpū (belly). In those moments, we did not concern ourselves with how much poi there was or if there would be enough for tomorrow. We did not wonder about who was going to Hawai'i next and would they bring us a bag of poi? We did not worry about getting another bag before we were 'ono (craving) for it. For in that moment, with the 'umeke (bowl) of poi in the center of the table, all that mattered was the love we shared with each other. I learned about waiwai (abundance) at the dinner table sharing poi with my family, aunties, uncles, and cousins. When I opened the lid of the poi bowl I was filled with aloha and waiwai.

Poi as Pedagogy

As a professor of Native Hawaiian and Indigenous politics, I strive to find new ways of decolonizing the academy. For the first time, I structured my graduate seminar to begin with a "aloha circle" and end with a "mahalo circle." I learned this practice of ho'owaiwai (creating abundance) from Ho'oulu 'Āina, a land-based community health care center that is part of Kōkua Kalihi Valley, a comprehensive health services center for the underserved community of Kalihi. The aloha circle reminds us that 'āina is a co-participant in all that we do and it asks each person in the circle to set their intentions for the work ahead of the group. At the end of class we stand in a circle again, holding hands, for the mahalo circle. Here we each give thanks for something we learned or appreciated from our work together. These moments are powerfully and emotionally transformative because in this space we renew individual commitments to our families, communities and lāhui while also giving thanks for waiwai in all its forms.[2]

On February 18, 2015 class began with an aloha circle. We stood, clasped hands and went around the circle sharing our names, the person we brought with us to class, and our individual intentions for class. At its conclusion, the student in charge of discussion began her presentation and then led us in the discussion of the readings. During this class session, students began to answer a question they had been asking all semester, "How do we put these theories into practice?" The discussion finally focused on how each of us could put the ideas presented in our readings on Indigenous resurgence into practice on a daily basis. At the conclusion of class we decided to use the mahalo circle to commit to engaging in an everyday act of resurgence that we could enact over the course of the week. The following week we reported on how we did during the aloha circle. A Samoan student born and raised on Oʻahu's North Shore committed to speaking Samoan with her younger sisters, two Kānaka ʻŌiwi students committed to speak ʻōlelo Hawaiʻi with their families who also speak ʻōlelo Hawaiʻi. Another student committed to decolonizing his diet by giving up white sugar, flour and soda. I committed to having a bowl of poi on my table.

On my way home from work that night I drove by a local supermarket and looked for the poi. I found the iconic bag of Taro Brand poi stacked on a shelf between the refrigerated poke case and the local food case, I made sure to buy two bags, which would get me to Friday or Saturday when I could buy poi from small family run kalo farms.

I was so excited to arrive home with my bags of poi. But my kids were less enthusiastic. My three kids, all born in Honolulu and growing up in Mānoa valley, have a very different relationship to poi. Poi has been a part of their diet since they were babies; it was the first solid food we fed them. We buy poi on a regular basis. They can have it whenever they want. They can taste the difference between the sweetness of the Kāʻī variety used to make the Hanalei brand of poi from Kauaʻi and the Lehua variety used to make the poi in the Taro Brand that is manufactured on Oʻahu. They know the texture and taste of paʻiʻai (pounded kalo before water is added) and how it differs from poi. Hāloa, kalo, paʻiʻai, poi are an integral part of their lives and yet we do not keep a ʻumeke of poi on our table.

In committing to placing the ʻumeke of poi on my table I invited my Tūtū and Kūkū to the table to share stories and life lessons. Sitting around a table with the ʻumeke at the center is an opportunity for trans-generational learning, the knowledge of kūpuna (grandparents) is passed to children, where we are reminded that Hāloa is our elder brother. My Tūtū and Kūkū passed away before my children were born. Bringing the ʻumeke of poi to the table gave me an opportunity to pass on the stories and life lessons they shared with me when I was a child.

Kūkū said:

"Eat from the center, don't dirty the side of the bowl."

"Clean your spoon before you put it in the bowl."

"Share! Keep the bowl in the center of the table where everyone can reach."

"Clean the sides before you close the bowl after eating."

"When the poi bowl is open [uncovered] we talk only about good things, we do not talk stink about others; this is the time to enjoy the food and the company of others."

This commitment to an everyday act of resurgence forced me rethink how our family eats poi. We typically serve the kids poi in separate bowls. Since they do not have to share, they didn't learn the lessons my Kūkū taught me. During the week the 'umeke came to the table my husband and I were able to share our stories and teach our kids important lessons.

Committing to the 'umeke of poi also made visible the challenges small kalo farmers face. When we returned to class the following week, I confessed that I fell short of my goal. I was not able to get to the local co-op in Honolulu in time to purchase poi made by small family run farms and I also did not make it to the farmers market to buy pa'i'ai and poi. Since my plan was to buy poi from small farmers over the weekend, I ran out before the week was up. The fact that I can only purchase homestead poi one day a week at the local co-op or drive thirty minutes to the windward side of the island is a reminder that eating poi it is still about availability and access—farmers' access to land, availability of fresh water, and access to consumer markets. For one week in February, poi was pedagogy. Each time the 'umkeke comes to the table we invite our kūpuna to join us.

NOTES
[1] We called my paternal grandmother, Tūtū, and my paternal grandfather Kūkū. The difference in spelling does not reflect gendered differences in the Hawaiian words but my family's use of the terms.
[2] Words cannot express my mahalo to Puni Freitas, the Director of Ho'oulu 'Āina, and the entire Ho'oulu 'Āina staff for their gifts of aloha and waiwai. For more information about Ho'oulu 'Āina see their website at http://www.hoouluaina.com/

The SX̱OLE (Reef Net Fishery) as an everyday act of Resurgence

NICK XEMŦOLTW̱ CLAXTON

ACCORDING TO WESTERN HISTORY, my people, the W̱SÁNEĆ People, have been living on their traditional territory on southern Vancouver Island and the Gulf and San Juan Islands for many thousands of years. According to W̱SÁNEĆ oral history, our existence here goes back to the very beginning — to the time of creation. Embedded in the landscape, and expressed through our language, stories and place names are the laws, beliefs and teachings that were given to us by XÁLs (the Creator). This is an important consideration, because the way our ancestors viewed and related to the world in traditional times is very different from the way we view the world in contemporary times.

Everyday acts of resurgence are about relating to the land in the ways of the ancestors. It is important to remember, share and live these teachings everyday. The revitalization and resurgence of the W̱SÁNEĆ Reef Net fishery – which is the W̱SÁNEĆ method to fish for salmon in very specific locations using a net that is suspended between two canoes and anchored behind a lead which funnels schools of salmon into the net – is a good example of an everyday act of resurgence through relating to the natural world through practice.

Thinking, acting and relating to our territories in ancestral ways should be fundamental to the healing of our communities, through the revitalization and resurgence of ancestral knowledge's and practices. Marie Battiste, Mi'kmaw educator and scholar states that we are "marinated in eurocentrism" through what she calls Cognitive Imperialism.[1] This eurocentrism actually causes us to be and keeps us disconnected from our homelands in our hearts, minds and spirits. Alternatively, ancestral worldviews fostered a deep relationship to our territories, as if we were related to the natural world. Viewing salmon, trees, or other elements of the natural world as relatives is what Enrique Salmón calls a "kincentric ecology". As Indigenous peoples, we need to look at, and relate to the natural world around us everyday, as if we are all relatives. For the W̱SÁNEĆ peoples, the Reef Net technology is a perfect example.

In understanding the Reef Net as more than just a fishing method, but as a rich cultural and spiritual practice, we must start with the oral history of it's origins. The following is a story that was shared with me by my late Uncle YEL̵ḴÁT̵TE (Dr. Earl Claxton Sr.) It is a belief of the W̱SÁNEĆ people that the SX̱OLE, the reef net, originated the following way:

A W̱SÁNEĆ couple had a beautiful and eligible young daughter. The family travelled together to ĆEȽTENEM to visit their relatives who lived there. While they were there, the young lady would often go sit alone on the shore and look out over the ocean. One evening, a young man came walking along the beach, and he spoke to the beautiful young W̱SÁNEĆ lady. After that first meeting, they met one another down at the shore many times and they became fond of each other.

The handsome young man wanted the young W̱SÁNEĆ princess to run away with him, so they could be together forever. Though the young W̱SÁNEĆ princess also wanted to be with the handsome young man, she was a strong believer in W̱SÁNEĆ traditions, and she told the young man that he must speak to her parents first and get their approval. The young man respected her wish and he spoke to her parents. The parents accepted the young man, but only if he stayed with the W̱SÁNEĆ people for a time. It was during this time, that the salmon became very scarce, and hard to catch. The W̱SÁNEĆ people began to suffer.

The young man offered his help to the W̱SÁNEĆ people. He asked them to bring him some SX̱OLE. This was a word that the W̱SÁNEĆ people had never heard before. They noticed that this young man spoke differently, and had many different names for the things he spoke of. No one knew that he was really speaking in spiritual terms, using sacred prayer words. They only knew that they had never heard those words before.

The young man requested many items with which he promised would help provide for W̱SÁNEĆ people. He requested a certain plant, and again the W̱SÁNEĆ people did not know what he was asking for. The W̱SÁNEĆ people brought the young man boughs, branches, roots, he rejected them all one by one, until one of them brought the pacific willow bush. The young man took the willow bush, and he stripped it of its inner bark. From this fibrous inner bark, he made cordage and began to construct a net.

The young man completed constructing the reef net gear with all of the other natural materials brought to him previously. He taught the W̱SÁNEĆ people the names of all of the different parts of the net and all of the terms used while fishing with the net. He taught the W̱SÁNEĆ people how to be reef net fishermen. The W̱SÁNEĆ people became successful in catching salmon, and became a prosperous people once again. The W̱SÁNEĆ people used the reef net, which was the gift of that young man, to catch salmon ever since then.

A short time later, the young man told the W̱SÁNEĆ people that it was time for him to take his new bride home with him. With all of their possessions loaded into their canoe, they departed, with the *young princess's family watching from the shore. The young man and the young woman, headed out to the deep water, and when they reached a distance away, they simply vanished into the water. It is now believed that the young man who came to W̱SÁNEĆ and married this young W̱SÁNEĆ princess was the spirit of the salmon in human form. He gave the W̱SÁNEĆ people the gift of their own way of fishing, and the W̱SÁNEĆ people gave him the gift of a beautiful wife.*

It is a belief of the W̱SÁNEĆ people that the salmon are our relatives, and they were people just like us, and they must be respected as such. The W̱SÁNEĆ people have fished this way for a very long time, and this is what connects us to the Salmon people.

This story of the Reef Net encompasses the significance and importance of the Reef Net Fishery of the W̱SÁNEĆ People. It reflects the beliefs of the W̱SÁNEĆ people and how we relate to the land and to the salmon. The Reef Net Fishery is our way of life, or connection to our territory; it formed the spiritual, social, physical and philosophical core and backbone of W̱SÁNEĆ traditional society. In the summer of 2014, the W̱SÁNEĆ people brought the SX̱OLE forward through a sacred ceremony, and then went fishing at an ancestral fishing location at Pender Island, for the first time in about 100 years. Through this Reef Net resurgence effort the W̱SÁNEĆ Nation also renewed relational and community ties with the W̱ŁEMI Nation. The W̱ŁEMI Nation fishermen and leadership also attending the W̱SÁNEĆ Reef Net ceremony in 2014, and then the summer of 2015 the W̱SÁNEĆ Reef Net fishermen attended a W̱ŁEMI naming ceremony at a shared ancestral Reef Net location on the San Juan Islands. The Reef Net has brought the W̱SÁNEĆ and the W̱ŁEMI Nations together on a resurgent journey back to the Reef Net fishery.

While this is oral history, and it is often told as a story, it also fosters belief system and way of viewing the world. When our elders share this story, it is believed to have actually happened. It did actually happen. It is a record of an actual historical occurrence. It also reflects an important philosophy, that we are directly related to the salmon. This is an important idea for W̱SÁNEĆ peoples, that we are related to our natural world. This denotes a particular relationship and responsibility to the natural world. This is a worldview that needs to be brought forward, taught, fostered in our children, and lived in an everyday way. This revitalization of the Reef Net knowledge has begun, and continues daily in our community Tribal high school. A Reef Net curriculum has been implemented this academic year, and efforts are being made to incorporate the Reef Net technology across all of the subjects taught in our high school. Through this everyday resurgence effort, the minds and identities of the W̱SÁNEĆ youth are being recentered on the Reef Net technology.

The Reef Net as resurgence, as a practice helps the W̱SÁNEĆ people to restore our physical, and spiritual presence on the land and water of our territory. There are now 10 new W̱SÁNEĆ Reef Net fishermen (myself included), who now know how it feels to fish in this ancestral way. Some of these new fishermen had never been to Pender Island before this act of resurgence. It also rebuilds our relationship to the salmon people, in traditional ways, particularly by nourishing the W̱SÁNEĆ people again physically and spiritually. The Reef Net practice has also brought generations, communities and families together. Moving forward with the Reef Net resurgence will help to transmit practical, cultural and spiritual knowledge across the generations once again. By doing this, over the long term, it is my vision that it will also start to rebuild and strengthen familial structures and W̱SÁNEĆ social and governance structures. In traditional times, the Reef net was also the core of W̱SÁNEĆ land-based economy, and it is hoped that it can once again grow to be that once again. By living and thinking in a W̱SÁNEĆ Reef Net paradigm, there is a real opportunity for the W̱SÁNEĆ people to look backward while moving forward to a much better future as a W̱SÁNEĆ people and nation.

Metaphorically, it is time to draw in our net together, and be nourished with the catch. It will strengthen our communities, to once again be with the salmon on the water as the salt water people. It is time to reacquaint ourselves with the Salmon people. We need to remember that a W̱SÁNEĆ princess bestowed upon us the gift of the W̱SÁNEĆ Reef Net fishery, and we must honour this gift every day, and allow it to draw out of our people, the W̱SÁNEĆ way. The Reef Net is a blessing, a beautiful W̱SÁNEĆ practice, and an everyday act of resurgence.

NOTES

[1] Battiste, Marie. 2013. Decolonizing Education: Nourishing the Learning Spirit. Saskatoon: Purich Publishing, p. 159.
[2] Salmón, Enrique. 2000. "Kincentric Ecology: Indigenous Perceptions of the Human-Nature Relationship". Ecological Applications, 10(5), 1327-1332.

Evading the Neo/colonial State Without Running to the Hills

Nearly-Illegal Food Harvesting in Aotearoa

BRAD COOMBES
(KATIMAMOE, NGATI KAHUNGUNU)

F OR DECADES, I EVADED SELF-IDENTIFICATION AS A LAWYER. While I recognize the emancipatory work that legal professionals can accomplish, I do not include my law degree on my business card and only raise that training in acts of revealingly self-deprecating humour. The shame reflects a deepening suspicion of law as a colonizing order, but it also flows from experience that neither grand courtroom deliberation nor any other form of extraordinary discourse is likely to sustain what is important for Maori. Conversely, I have also come to recognise the limitations of bellicose protest, blatantly illegal activities and other attempts to dismantle neo/colonialism through acts of belligerence. Hence, this think-piece is my homage to the subversive activities of Maori that inhabit the space between what society deems legal and illegal, for it is such everyday and not spectacular practices that most inconvenience the neo/colonial state.

According to James C. Scott, the *Art of not being governed* is grounded in daily practices of apparent disorder that make subaltern peoples unintelligible to the monitoring and calculating functions of the state.[1] Scott emphasises strategic self-denial of the recording, categorisation and translation of cultural practices. He has been criticised for over-emphasis on such strategic illegibility as one of potentially many strategies by which Indigenous peoples disrupt neo/colonialism.[2] While he has proven the relevance of everyday resistance to an extent achieved by no other academic, his framing of cultural endurance is based rather too heavily on Indigenous *evasion* of colonial rule. To delimit Indigenous activism to f(l)ight is to undervalue how, for instance, daily enactment of the *nearly*-illegal can so undermine colonial rationality as to prompt its transformation. Here, I argue that Maori defiance towards the criminalization of cultural harvests so unsettles state regulators that it generates new and significant concessions. While the regressive incrementalism of rights discourse may not sustain Indigenous resurgence, concessions enacted through state embarrassment as opposed to those which flow from the state's management of protest may prompt important moments of societal re-evaluation. Clandestine acts of minor, often involuntary offending are an important means through which Indigenous peoples unsettle the fiction of absolute colonial erasure. They routinize disparate acts into the fortifying momentum of indigeneity, and problematize the universalising assumptions and regulatory apparatus of the colonial state. Because the following vignettes involve somewhat illegal practices, I have chosen to avoid proper- and place-names.

DISCOMFITURE BY ROTARY HOE

Recently, I was engaged to represent an elderly Maori man in an out-of-court arbitration that, had its outcome been different, would have resulted in significant fines and the loss of his house and savings. Inadvertently, he had been contravening regional plan and fisheries rules for several decades. His sin was to care for shellfisheries that had sustained Maori communities for centuries. While it is legal to harvest those shellfish and whereas daily limits for personal use are generous, encouraging their growth and abundance through unauthorized forms of active management may contravene the law. The Eurocentric emphasis on preservationism understands nature as something best left untouched, but the elder understood that turning over and thinning shellfish beds were essential *obligations* that promoted healthy growth dynamics. Since the 1980s, rural depopulation of his homelands had reduced the benevolent disturbance upon which healthy shellfisheries are dependent. Yet, new technology and some ingenuity provided useful substitutes: the elder purchased and modified a petrol-driven rotary hoe that is marketed for domestic gardeners. During the next 32 years, he walked onto the sand flats at most low tides and "turned over a rugby field's worth or so" of shellfish habitat, returning to each site at least twice a year. Since 1995, such activities contravened regional plan rules that require a resource consent for disturbing or removing more than a cubic metre of sand. Those rules were never intended to regulate harvesting nor management of shellfish, but rather they were established to control commercial extraction of sand and dispersal of sediment.

Notwithstanding that his personal form of shellfisheries management was unnoticed for such a long time and that he had produced the largest and most abundant pipi, tuatua and tuangi known to all parties involved, discovery of his practices led to a formal notice of abatement. Yet, the prospect of public empathy towards an 82 year old thrown before the courts encouraged state officials to pursue out-of-court arbitration. At all stages, the elder presented a convincing argument: shellfish had sustained his people for hundreds of years and he was therefore obliged to tend the beds. After all, his disturbance regime was clearly benefitting indigenous species of importance. Although refusing to commit to any change in that regime, he was cautioned and not fined. He returned to his work the next day, but now with an audience of media representatives and state environmental monitors. Each new iteration of arbitration attracts new monitoring and additional reporting in the media, but the state has no resolve to prosecute him further, rendering its regulations more broadly ineffectual. In the large harbour in which he works, the elder is now joined by seven others who have purchased and modified rotary hoes for similar acts of tolerated but essentially illegal work. While the state can absorb the blatantly illegal through punitive coercion, it may be so embarrassed by the *almost*-legal and by elders who can finesse the fine line of public opinion that it comes to accept the contradictions in its own rules. For local Maori, achieving substitution of legal strictures by *de facto* rights heralded a significant act of cultural maintenance, but it was not predicated on any self-displacement to evade the state's reach.

NGA MANU O NGA WAIRUA E RERE

In Waitangi Tribunal evidence I wrote for one tribe, I detailed how customary harvests of native birds were criminalized in most parts of Aotearoa by 1912. In a landlocked forest enclave of the North Island, that presented a significant dilemma for its denizens who had limited access to alternative forms of protein. One hundred years later, their dilemma had shifted: bird populations continued to decline because invasive species and loss of habitat were more consequential than the impact of customary harvests. Yet, *pakeha* assumptions that the *tangata whenua* regularly poached native species had impacted on the latter's *mana* and public reputation. Reverence for the birds that had once sustained them as *kai* meant that few if any locals were responsible for poaching and, indeed, the tribe had since become renowned for its conservation of kiwi (the 'national' bird) and kereru (a wood pigeon). In the opinion of elders, non-local Maori were responsible for clandestine acts of poaching. As tangata whenua had no opportunity to exercise legally their mana through bird harvests, there were few local rights within the area that outsiders could observe and respect, so the latter filled a *mana*-void with their own harvesting practices. Revealingly, they also disregarded the solely legal authority of the Department of Conservation (DoC) to control historically important resources.

Local elders met with DoC staff and with elders of tribes that surround their forests. They proposed a bold but illegal solution. They would recommence harvests of kereru, but only to provide the last meal for elders before departure of their *wairua* to other realms. Representatives of DoC comprehended the secondary intent of that strategy to regulate the actions of *non-local* Maori, but they also noted that reestablishment of harvests contravened many of its standard operating procedures and several acts of parliament. Of note, though, many DoC staff in the area are themselves Maori, and some of their pakeha colleagues are married to Maori women. Although they had universal(ising) obligations to the law and their Department, they too were enmeshed within the everyday, working amidst the daily routines that sustain relationships with friends, relatives and neighbors. Although they refused to sanction officially any harvests, they agreed to turn a postcolonial blind eye to the work of the elders. Since that time, only six birds have been harvested to become last meals of the almost departed. Signs of poaching are not evident because all Maori including those who are not local recognize the mana of the local elders to maintain the ritual of feeding ancestral kai to those about to pass. Subsequently, young, old, local and non-local Maori, along with DoC and many pakeha organisations have intensified their efforts to control exotic predators and competitors within local forests. Any evasion in this instance has been limited to DoC staff; tangata whenua have usurped the law without needing to evade its spatial scope, as they have exploited the difference between official power and the practical reality of *the law in-place*.

Nearly-illegal but everyday activities and illegal yet occasional practices can render the colonial state and its legal devices irrelevant by means that do not require grandiose constitutional reform nor running for the hills.

NOTES

[1] James C. Scott, 2009, *The Art of Not Being Governed: An Anarchist History of Upland Southeast Asia*, New Haven: Yale University Press.

[2] Sanford F. Schram, 2012, The artful study of not being governed: Better political science for a better world, *Common Knowledge* 18(3): 528-37.

[3] Bengt G. Karlsson, 2013, Evading the state: Ethnicity in northeast India through the lens of James Scott, *Asian Ethnology* 72(2): 321-31.

[4] Taiaiake Alfred, 2009, Colonialism and state dependency, *Journal of Aboriginal Health* 5(2): 42-60.

Intimate acts of resurgence

witnessing the resistance of indigenous children and youth from the personal to the Indigisphere and beyond

NATALIE CLARK

"Mom I know what you do. You don't think I know history, I do. Why would you be a social worker? How does that help children?"
—Cohen Clark, age 9, Secwepemc

PRESENT IN THIS QUESTION from my twin son Cohen is the everyday acts of resurgence of children and youth within intimate relationships and spaces, and the revealed practices of naming and questioning the harms done to Indigenous children and youth through colonial systems, in this case social work. This chapter will theorize the processes and practices of listening and witnessing the everyday truth-telling and resurgence of our children and youth and to attend to the shape and quality of the shifting sites where this happens. I will be focusing on the witnessing from within intimate spaces of relationship as a mother and will share examples woven from the spaces I move through with my children from the intimate and familial of birth, to the resurgence spaces of ceremony. In all of these spaces I argue, Indigenous children and youth are engaged in intimate and daily acts of decolonizing.

My son texted me while I was writing this paper, asking when I was born and about a significant event in my life. I responded, 1968, the year of my birth, and when I became a mother – when you all came. This was a process of convergence, of centrifugal forces- pushing in and out, the resulting forces, or processes emerge at specific times, places, and in relation to specific people. This unique coming together is also defined by the moving in and out of spaces that also define the processes of emergence and resurgence. Mothering has shaped me, brought me teachers, and deepened and changed my witnessing practice.

cteksle7íl't – to give birth to twins: *Twin stories*

The Secwepemc ontology and worldview, and my relationship to them, can also be found within stories about twins and the ceremonies and meanings associated with them. As the mother of Secwepemc twins I had often been told the twin stories from the Nation, and had dreamed of Grizzly bear during my pregnancy. These stories continued to be told in spite of their suppression by colonial researchers such as James Teit and Boas.[1]

In contrast to the powerful stories told me to of birthing Secwepemc twins, my own experience within the colonial system was one marked by risk. I remember when my twins were born, they chose to come a month early into this world, and I a solo parent was home alone with my daughter when my water broke. Living in Vancouver, we were far away from home in Secwepemc territory. Jimi Hendrix played in the truck that my friend Emily's boyfriend of the time drove me to the hospital in. I remember him saying "it would be so fucking cool if you gave birth right now". I arrived at the hospital, with a man not the father of my children and was met by another man, a dear friend, a Jewish rabbi and midwife. The nurses looked to both of these men as fathers, to which we all laughed and shook our heads. Later, after Tyee and Cohen come into this world – I am in the room recovering and the social worker comes in. I know her. I even hired her and trained her. I work at this very hospital as a youth health consultant where I develop curriculum for doctors and nurses to better meet the needs of "vulnerable" youth. I am surprised to see her.

"K. what are you doing here?" She becomes visibly distressed – and then says they sent her. Indigenous solo parent of twins – the box was checked somewhere-the risk box – I was in it and had not requested to be there. I sent her away – we both laughed, but this story stays with me still. How do I respond to the violence in that room, in that moment from a friend – violence written onto my children's small bodies – coating them with risk and need before they are even a few hours old? I contrast this story with the sacred stories of birthing twins that I received in community – stories that blanketed them in power and place.

Grounding in our Own Experience: Reflexivity and Resurgence

An essential part of witnessing practice is to see our children and youth, and to hear them – to enact our obligation to them, and to place them in the centre of our circle. I suggest that a first step in Witnessing Practice is to begin with ourselves, with our bodies and with our relationships to the lands, and the Nation where we are located - what I call "Grounding in Our Own Experience".

As described by George Manuel (1974) Secwepemc chief and international Indigenous rights activist, in his book *The Fourth World*, "the residential schools were the laboratory and production line of the colonial system" convert to endnote – not in works cited(p. 63). Perhaps the greatest loss was the breaking of the sacred place of children in the kinship circle, and in many cases their spirit through the loss of language and ceremony and the resulting loss of the raising up of children as researchers. Secwepemc Elder Dr. Mary Thomas (2001) states that, "in comparison with the way I grew up, we were always asking questions: "Grandma, what is this? Grandma, what are you doing? Grandma, why do you want it? All those questions. We were allowed to talk as much as we could" endnote(p. 24). In stark contrast, Thomas describes the silencing of residential school, and I would argue that this silencing was also of the inherent researcher or questioner in every child. In returning to the question of my son Cohen that began this paper – I suggest that we must engage with our own experiences of truth-telling, of naming, and of resistance in order to stand with our children and witness their questions.

I am inspired by the practice of naming and noticing of Leanne Simpson in her keynote address for the Indigenous Women's Symposium (2011) where she names the invisible work of mothering and grandmothering. "I thought about all the hard work that went on over just the past week in this community that was done by Anishinaabekwewag – the teaching, the mothering and grandmothering... And I thought about how all of that hard work, and how for the most part it goes completely unrecognized and too often completely un-noticed. And so I think what I want to say tonight is that this week, I noticed. This week I paid attention and it was overwhelming the sacrifices and the love that I witnessed from all the Anishinaabekwewag."

How can we listen with the respect of June Jordan and attend to the noticing as Leanne Simpson does, invoking our "MotherING" as a site of resistance, a "political site" to enact social justice endnote(Gumbs, 2016:22).

Below are some reflection questions that I offer:

- *What is my own embodied experience of witnessing, testimony in   my family, community, and culture?*
- *Who has been the witness to my stories as a child, youth, and now? Disclosures? What did I need?*
- *How are these stories affecting my body and my knowing?*
- *What fear/hopes do I have about receiving questions, truth-telling from my children or other children, youth in my life?*
- *What stories of resistance, survivance have inspired me?*
- *How authentic am I in my relationships with my children? With colleagues? With others? What part(s) of me are not present?*
- *What practices and processes will support collectives of caring and mothering in our homes and communities?*

It is vitally important in our listening and our witnessing that we do not continue to create narratives of risk and harm separated from the stories of strength, resiliency and survivance.

In our Indigenous family and community contexts we weave and tell stories of violence, resistance, and healing. We are telling in order not only to share about the violence, but also to change it. It is vitally important that we see and honor our Indigenous children/youth as truth-tellers, knowledge makers and and activists.

I would like to end this paper with a poem I wrote when I was asked to be a keynote at an Indigenous youth conference – and I wanted to speak of my own acts of resistance as a youth to the risk written on my body. I offer this poem to my son Cohen in response to his question, and as a way of resisting the risk written on my body as a young woman.

Basket
Ball
Hoop dancer
A pair of green high-tops lost
Most improved player
Red high-tops stolen
Removed
Beyond risk
Do not tell me of your fear for me
If you do not share your hope

My gifts hidden from you
By the old small pox blanket you have draped over me
Woven of my risk and statistics of harm

You cannot see beyond lives lived now
Leaders of today
Not tomorrow
I remember the story of this on my body

Basketball coach whispers words while draping the blanket
I feel sorry for you, sorry for you as a child of a single parent, on welfare
Punched me

No Air

Wrapped me in the small pox blanket of your words woven of pity of shame dipped

in risk
I could not
Did not recognize myself

Anger. How dare you. I threw the blanket off – marching off to see the counselor for the one and only time I did in school.

His words – Go now. Get him out of whatever class he is in and tell him how he made you feel.

Moment frozen – staring at him teaching through the school door, small window frozen in time.

Truth-telling. I know more and deeper than any of these privileged kids. How Dare you? I refuse this blanket you have made for me woven of your stories of single moms and wild child. I hand it back to you. But not without the gift of my own blanket. I can sink a three pointer, and I am much more than your story of me.

Pride. Resistance. Resistance. Survivance. Poem by Natalie Clark November 2015

NOTES

[1] They are the only stories that Teit gathered through interviewing a female Elder, XwElinEk and yet these stories were suppressed by Teit and Boas along with any references to the sacred role of grizzly and women in the twin stories and ceremonies (Wickwire, 2001 convert sources to endnotes). Wickwire, W. (2001). The Grizzly Gave Them the Song: James Teit and Franz Boas Interpret Twin Ritual in Aboriginal British Columbia, 1897-1920. The American Indian Quarterly Volume 25, Number 3, Summer 2001 pp. 431-452.

Ua pā i ka leo

The power of our Native voices to enact and inspire Indigenous resurgence

MAYA L. KAWAILANAOKEAWAIKI SAFFERY

I T WAS A WARM, CLEAR DAY at Kailua beach on October 16, 2013. On such a beautiful day, one would expect to see one of the most popular Oʻahu beaches covered with flowery beach towels and Tommy Bahama lounge chairs; the water full of ABC store boogie boards ridden awkwardly by sunscreen soaked foreigners; the outer reefs and small islets cluttered with countless schools of brightly-colored kayaks rented by the hour; and the sky distorted by the kites of surfers speeding through the waves and launching themselves into the air. Unfortunately, when residents and visitors think of Kailua today, these are the images that usually come to mind. They do not typically think of Kailua as a site of Hawaiian resurgence, but on that particular afternoon in October that is exactly what I was a part of.

That Wednesday in 2013 marked the second time in history that the waʻa kaulua or Hawaiian double-hulled voyaging canoe Hōkūleʻa[1] sailed into Kailua (an ahupuaʻa or traditional land division in the district of Koʻolaupoko on the island of Oʻahu). As a kupa (Native) of this ahupuaʻa and a practitioner of traditional hula who received my hula training in this ahupuaʻa, I helped plan and oversee the hosting of Hōkūleʻa and her crew for several days by our Kailua Hawaiian community. The schedule of events began that day with an arrival ceremony at Kanukuokaʻelepulu (a portion of Kailua beach where Kaʻelepulu stream enters the sea). It was there on that clear, sunny day that a spontaneous exchange of aloha ʻāina (love for the land) oratory in Hawaiian langauge between two young Kānaka of Kailua took place. Their call and response only lasted about ten minutes, but the power of this everyday act of resurgence continues to echo and reverberate long after their initial words were spoken...ua pā i ka leo (to be struck by the voice). All of us who stood with them that day were immediately reminded of the power of our Native voices to enact and inspire Indigenous resurgence through our Native languages for the decolonization, re-culturation, and regeneration of ourselves and our communities.

With just enough wind to fill her sails, Hōkūleʻa sailed proudly into Kailua bay under her own power, around Mōkapu, passed Mōkōlea, through a natural channel in the reef, and close to shore where our group of cultural practitioners, community leaders, and school groups were waiting for them. After setting anchor, her crew was ferrried to the beach aboard canoes paddled by members of various Kailua canoe clubs and greeted with chant and lei by seven of Kailua's kumu hula (hula teachers). But before our guests emerged completely out of the water, one of the Kanaka orators mentioned earlier, crewmember Kaleomanuiwa (Kaleo) Wong, called out to the kamaʻāina (Native-born Kānaka) of Kailua (whose presence is often forgotten or erased by locals and foreigners alike), asking their permission to come ashore. This is an excerpt from his speech.

> E ke kamaʻāina, eia lā he waʻa, he kaulua i pae mai nei
> He nonoi kēia e pae ka waʻa
> E kamaʻāina ka waʻa iā Kailua
> E kamaʻāina ʻo Kailua i ka waʻa
> He welina, he leo aloha wale nō kēia[2]

On behalf of his hoa waʻa (crewmembers), Kaleo addressed the kamaʻāina of Kailua, including those Kānaka physically on the beach as well as the kūpuna (ancestors) of Kailua, seen and unseen, who were also there to bear witness to this historic event. He recognized their presence and depth of knowledge by delivering his words directly to them, speaking only in ʻōlelo Hawaiʻi (Hawaiian language), and recounting the genealogies of both the waʻa kaulua who brought them there and the land who now welcomed them. He had no doubt that his hosts would be able to understand every poetic saying he referenced, recognize every ancestral name he honored, and appreciate the intention behind every word he spoke. And he was right. After listing the islands that Hōkūleʻa had visited just prior to arriving in Kailua, he proclaimed, "Noke i ka holo a pae mai i ke one o Kākuhihewa, ka heke o nā moku." (Hōkūleʻa continued to sail until landing on the sands of Kākuhihewa (Oʻahu), the best of all islands). This passionate statement engendered exclamations of pride from throughout the crowd. When he recounted the names of Kailua's sacred places and ancestors like Alāla and Kūaliʻi, Kahinihiniʻula and Hauwahine, Pāmoa and Kākuhihewa, shouts of "eō" erupted from all around. It was as if he was calling out to these kūpuna and inviting them to participate in the ceremony, their presence thus demanding excellence and accountability from us all as we moved forward.

Upon the conclusion of Kaleo's eloquent address, one of the kamaʻāina of Kailua, Kahikina de Silva, responded with a speech of her own, welcoming Kaleo and the others to our kulāiwi (homeland, community) and inviting them to come ashore. This was not a pre-planned performance that she choreographed with Kaleo beforehand. It was a spontaneous interaction between two Kānaka who were reviving in that moment the cultural practice of Hawaiian oratory. In fact, this was probably the first time that this kind of exchange between guest and host in Hawaiian-language-only had been heard in public in Kailua for more than a century. Ua pā i ka leo—Kahikina was struck by Kaleo's speech and was inspired to respond on behalf of the rest of us kamaʻāina of Kailua. The result was an intertwining of words, names, genealogies, and histories that created a lei around us all, a lei that celebrated our presence as kupa of Kailua, as ʻŌiwi of Hawaiʻi.

Any time we speak ʻōlelo Hawaiʻi it is an act of resurgence because we are consciously choosing to give ea (life, breath) to the words of our kūpuna in our contemporary time. These words are intimately tied to our land- and water-based practices as well as the contexts in which these practices were developed. Our Native languages are a reflection of who we are, what we value, and how we understand and engage with the world. They are "animate and animating, [express] our living spirit through sound and the emotion with which we speak"[3], and their survival is intimately tied to the survival of our people.[4] The ability of the two orators to speak exclusively in ʻōlelo Hawaiʻi and the ability of most participants in the ceremony to understand their words with no English translation was also a powerful testament to the wealth of knowledge still held in Kailua and our steadfast commitment as cultural practitioners of Kailua to put this knowledge into practice. It actually set the tone for the rest of the weekend where crewmembers were engaged with members of a variety of Hawaiian organizations from Kailua who are working to fulfill their kuleana (responsibility, obligation) to our community through the stewardship of our sacred places, the cultivation of our Native foods and medicines, the restoration of our Native forests and wetlands, and the perpetuation of our many other cultural and spiritual practices.

This brief exchange of words between guest and host, a Kānaka from the sea and a Kānaka from the land, created a piko or convergence of ea—the life, breath, and sovereignty of the people and the land of Kailua—which required everyone there to ask themselves, "What is my relationship to this piko and how does my positionality define my kuleana to it?" The coming together of these two Hawaiian voices created "a space of storied presencing, alternative imaginings, transformation, reclamation—resurgence".[5] It was a celebration that, in spite of the invasion and occupation of our lands and waters by foreigners, we are still here. But we are not just present but thriving, ready to steward our lands and lead our community in envisioning a healthy and prosperous future for Kailua. Their actions that day and those they inspired in the weeks and months that followed directly challenge the settler narratives that discredit the current leadership, capacity, and integrity of the Kailua Hawaiian community.[6] We are not just ready to take care of our own lands and make decisions about how they should be stewarded; we are already doing so.

Right after Kaleo and Kahikina's oratory, as we all still stood in the sand and surf, my hula sisters and I presented a hula to the crew of Hōkūleʻa as a way to affirm and remind us all of this reality. The hula we offered, ʻŪlei Pahu i ka Moku, is a prophecy chant of loss, warning Hawaiians that if we do not holdfast to the steering paddle of our canoe [E ku i ta hoe uli], others will take it from us and the result will be, A he mea/A he mea ʻoe, translated by premier Hawaiian scholar Mary Kawena Pukui as, "You are nothing/You Hawaiians will be as nothing."[7] However, Patience Namaka Bacon (daughter of Tūtū Pukui who taught this hula to my kumu, Māpuana de Silva) gives us hope when she told my kumu that these final lines can also be interpreted as a question instead of a statement—Who are you? Will you let someone else define who you are and the direction your "waʻa" (canoe, community, etc.) will take you or will you take hold of the "hoe uli" (steering paddle), and navigate your own paths to ea (life, sovereignty, self-determination)? It is our choice. As exemplified by the words and actions of Kaleo, Kahikina, and the rest of us who participated in the hosting of Hōkūleʻa and her crew in 2013, there is no doubt that the Kānaka of Kailua have our hoe uli firmly in our hands and are navigating our waʻa towards a distant yet visible shoreline where our presence in Kailua is real, recognized, and resurging.

NOTES

[1] Hōkūleʻa was born from the sands of Hakipuʻu, Koʻolaupoko, Oʻahu and launched into the waters of Kāneʻohe bay on March 8, 1975. She became a symbol of Hawaiian excellence and hope for the future of our lāhui (nation) since the success of her first voyage from Hawaiʻi to Tahiti in 1976 using only the ocean swells, stars, sun, moon, clouds, and birds to guide her way. Before Hōkūleʻa, no double-hulled voyaging canoe had been built or navigated in the way of our ancestors for a few hundred years due in large part to centuries of occupation and colonization by American missionaries and their descendants. Since her first voyage in 1976, Hōkūleʻa has successfully traveled over 150,000 nautical miles and bridged over one hundred islands in the Pacific using non-instrument navigation. These traditional methods of navigation are rooted in the teachings of our ancestors but went unpracticed in Hawaiʻi for centuries until Pwo Navigator Pius Mau Piailug from the island of Satawal in Micronesia agreed to teach Hawaiians to sail like our kūpuna once again. Hōkūleʻa is currently on a voyage around the world to connect with other Indigenous communities and spread the message of Mālama Honua, caring for island Earth. Her continued success in the Pacific, and now across the globe has inspired the births of numerous waʻa throughout Hawaiʻi and Polynesia as well as the training of a new generation of voyagers and navigators, ensuring that the art and science of deep sea voyaging will never go to sleep again.

[2] My translation of this excerpt of Kaleo's speech:

To the children of this land/the native borns of Kailua/our hosts, here is a canoe, a double-hulled voyaging canoe that has just landed

This is a request to come ashore

The canoe shall become familiar to Kailua

And Kailua shall become familiar to the waʻa

This is a greeting, a voice of aloha

[3] Gregory Cajete, *Native Science: Natural Laws of Interdependence,* Clear Light Publishers, Santa Fe, NM, 72.

[4] A reference to 1) the wise saying, "I ka ʻōlelo nō ke ola. I ka ʻōlelo nō ka make. In language there is life. In language there is death." (Pukui, 1983, p. 129) and 2) a

newspaper article in the Hawaiian language newspaper *Puuhona o Na Hawaii* (January 26, 1917) about link between language and national identity.

[5] Leanne Simpson, *Dancing on Our Turtle's Back, Stories of Nishnaabeg Re-creation, Resurgence and a New Emergence*, Arbeiter Ring Publishing, Winnipeg, Manitoba, 2011, 96.

[6] For example, the Kailua Neighborhood Board and other loud settler residents of Kailua are trying to block a plan (HHF/DLNR Kawainui Revised Master Plan) that will allow Hawaiian cultural, spiritual, educational, and environmental organizations to have a permanent presence around Kawainui fishpond in the center of Kailua to fulfill our kuleana to our people, places, and practices.

[7] Kīhei de Silva, *Merrie Monarch Hula Festival Fact Sheet*, Unpublished Manuscript, 2004.

The Piko Æffect

MEGUMI CHIBANA

Gattin naran! *Hantai*!! No!!! ‘a‘ole!!!!

I have heard enough of these chanting slogans.
I have seen enough of these raised fists in the air.
I have had enough of these heats of anger.
I have felt enough of these energies behind silence.

ENOUGH to be oppressed, repressed, and depressed.
ENOUGH to burn myself out of confusion, frustration, and infuriation.
I had enough.

My tears are dried out for those unhealed wounds.
My throat is choked up for those worldless words.
My face twitches with tensions.
My heart bursts with pressures.
Was I haunted...? NO.

Don't tell me that I do nothing.
Don't tell me what I am doing is just "in school."
Don't tell me my research makes no change "in real life."
THIS is what I do.
THIS is what my ʻohana[1] shared with me.

"You know, our family is not rich. We don't have much property to leave you,
kids. But remember, study hard and see the world. Knowledge you gain, nobody
can take them away from you."

Yuru harasu funi ya ninufa bushi miati
Wan nacheru uya ya wandu miati[2]

So... I studied. Studied harder than I could've ever imagined in myself.

Listening to fading native voices with one ear, imperial speeches
with the other ear.
Looking at the changing landscape with one eye, thick books with the other eye.
My brain turned right and left, up and down, swirl around to digest them.

Finally, words came out of my mouth... no surprise.
Uchinaguchi, *Nihongo*, English, Pidgin, ʻōlelo Hawaiʻi... all mixed up.

Well, I may no can speak any of them "properly."
But I no worry.
I got choke[3] friends in the world who get dat.
I may not be a good "intellectual."
But I no worry.

I know these gentle smiles of *Obaachan*[4] when their native tongues get heard.
I know these proud voices of *keiki*[5] singing songs in *shima kutuba.*[6]
I know these passionate eyes of students wanting to learn more of *moʻolelo*[7] of
ʻāina[8] they live.
I know these tight hugs of my *shinkanuchā*[9] from wherever their pikos are.

So Mom, am I doing well enough of what you could not do?

NOTES

[1] Family in an extended sense (in 'ōlelo Hawai'i).

[2] A ship sailing at night, get its bearings from the North Star; My parents who gave me life, get their bearings from me (in Uchinaguchi/Okinawan).

[3] A lot (in Pidin).

[4] A grandmother and an elderly woman (in Japanese).

[5] A child (in 'ōlelo Hawai'i).

[6] Language of community (in Uchinaguchi).

[7] Story (in 'ōlelo Hawai'i).

[8] Land (in 'ōlelo Hawai'i).

[9] Fellows, friends, and comrades (in Uchinaguchi/Okinawan).

Everyday Acts of Resurgence

People, Places, Practices

biographies

HŌKŪLANI K. AIKAU (Kānaka ʻŌiwi) is an associate professor in the Division of Gender Studies and the Division of Ethnic Studies at the University of Utah. She has published two books: A Chosen People, a Promised Land: Mormonism and Race in Hawaiʻi (University of Minnesota Press, 2012) and Feminist Waves, Feminist Generational Cultures: Life Stories from Three Generations in the Academy, 1968-1998 (co-edited with Karla Erickson and Jennier L. Pierce, University of Minnesota Press, 2007). Her next full length monograph Hoaʻāina: Restoring People, Places and Practices is an ethnography of a wetland restoration project on in Heʻeia, Oʻahu. Her most important accomplishment is being mother to Sanoe, ʻĪmaikalani, and Hiʻilei.

GERALD TAIAIAKE ALFRED is from Kahnawá:ke in the Mohawk Nation. He is a Professor of Indigenous Governance and Political Science at the University of Victoria. He is the author of three books: Heeding the Voices of Our Ancestors and Peace, Power, Righteousness from Oxford University Press, and Wasáse: Indigenous Pathways of Action and Freedom, from the University of Toronto Press.

SHELBY BLACKJACK is an artist and cultural coordinator of Northern Tutchone ancestry. She is a member of Little Salmon Carmacks First Nation and of Wolf Clan heritage. Shelby received a Diploma of Fine Arts from Victoria College of Art in 2006. She received a Masters of Education in Leadership through Simon

Fraser University in 2014. She comes from a long line of artisans and storytellers, and loves to share the history behind the traditional art forms that she teaches.

LIANNE MARIE LEDA CHARLIE is Wolf Clan and a descendant of the Tagé Cho Hudän (Big River People), Northern Tutchone speaking people of the Yukon. She is the granddaughter of Leda Jimmy of Little Salmon River and Big Salmon Charlie of Big Salmon River on her dad's side and Donna Olsen of Denmark and Benjamin Larusson of Iceland on her mother's side. She was born in Whitehorse, Yukon to her mother, Luanna Larusson, and late father, Peter Charlie. Lianne is a Political Science instructor at Yukon Collage in Whitehorse, Yukon, and a PhD Candidate in Indigenous Politics Program at the University of Hawai`i at Mānoa.

MEGUMI CHIBANA was born and raised in Okinawa. Megumi is currently pursuing a PhD in Political Science at the University of Hawai'i at Mānoa. Her research interests are situated in the intersection of land use, agrarian movements, indigenous politics and culture in the Asia Pacific, and trans-indigenous approaches.

NICK CLAXTON's ancestral hereditary name is XEMŦOLTW̱. He is from the S,ŦÁUTW̱ Community of the W̱SÁNEĆ Nation. Nick received his Master's in Indigenous Governance and his PhD in Curriculum Studies from the University of Victoria, where he is currently an Assistant Teaching Professor in Indigenous Education Department.

NATALIE CLARK, M.S.W., PhD (abd). Natalie's practice, teaching and research over the last 20 years have focused on violence and trauma with children, youth and their families and communities and the coping responses to trauma and violence. Natalie's work is informed and mobilized through her interconnected identities including her metis ancestry; as a solo-parent of three Secwepmec children and part of the Secwepemc community; an academic; activist and sexual abuse counsellor. Natalie Clark is on faculty in the school of social work at TRU where her research and practice is informed by Indigenous methodologies, intersectionality and critical participatory action research in the area of youth health, trauma, Indigenous health, and education.

BRAD COOMBES is an instructor and researcher at the School of Environment, University of Auckland, Aotearoa/New Zealand. Kati Mamoe and Ngati Kahungunu are his iwi (tribes). A geographer and lawyer by training, he researches at the interface between indigenous livelihoods, political ecology and environmental justice, and regularly contributes to the Waitangi Tribunal's settlement process for Maori land and resource claims.

JEFF KANOHALIDOH CORNTASSEL is a writer, teacher and father from the Tsalagi (Cherokee) Nation. He is currently Associate Professor and Director of Indigenous Governance at the University of Victoria located on the unceded ancestral homelands of the Lekwungen and Wsanec peoples. In 2016-17, Corntassel was awarded the Sequoyah Fellow at Northeastern State University in Tahlequah, Oklahoma. His research and teaching interests focus on "Everyday Acts of Resurgence" and the intersections between sustainable self-determination, community resurgence, climate change and well-being, and Indigenous political mobilization. Jeff's work has been published in Alternatives, Decolonization, American Indian Quarterly, Human Rights Quarterly, and Social Science Journal.

A deeply hyphenated Hawaiian, **KĪHEI DE SILVA** is Hilo-born, Kailua-raised, Kamehameha-confused, and Pomona-educated. He is, on his mother's side, a bone-keeper of Hōnaunau and, on his father's, a birth-stone caretaker of Kūkaniloko. He writes new songs to which better ears have put music, and he writes about older songs that he might not, in truth, understand. He has been a teacher of high school English and not done those kids irreparable harm. He rides mock-heroically on his wife Māpuana's coattails; his best students are hers and his daughters with her. He would always rather be cleaning yard at home and at Ulupō. Or word-playing with his granddaughter 'Ula.

SENKA ERIKSEN is a PhD student in the Indigenous Governance program at the University of Victoria. Her research centers on decolonial processes through critical analysis of past, present and future directions of settler presence. She focuses on everyday acts of solidarity, emergent relationships to Indigenous lands and waters, and the generation of spaces for Indigenous resurgence and self-determination.

ERYNNE M. GILPIN is a Saulteaux-Cree Métis PhD candidate with the Indigenous Governance Program at the University of Victoria and a Graduate Student Fellow at the Centre for Global Studies. Her Master's project (SSHRC funded) was with the Tsartlip Garden Project in community efforts of food sovereignty and land-based education pedagogies. Today, her Doctoral work (SSHRC funded) focuses on Indigenous wellness, leadership and body-governance; specifically birth-work.

NOELANI GOODYEAR-KA'ŌPUA is a Kanaka Maoli educator, teacher and organizer. She works as an Associate Professor of Indigenous and Hawaiian Politics at the University of Hawai'i. Her research focuses on documenting, analyzing and proliferating the ways people are transforming imperial and settler colonial relations through Indigenous political values and initiatives. Her books include The Seeds We Planted: Portraits of a Native Hawaiian Charter School (University of Minnesota Press, 2013), A Nation Rising: Hawaiian Movements for Life, Land and Sovereignty (Duke University Press, 2014), and The Value of Hawai'i, 2: Ancestral Roots, Oceanic Visions. Find more about her writings, curriculum and other projects at www.noegoodyearkaopua.com.

TRICIA DIBIKGEEZHIGOKWE MCGUIRE-ADAMS is an Assistant Lecturer in the Faculties of Kinesiology, Sport, & Recreation and Natives Studies at the University of Alberta. She belongs to Bingwi Neyaashi Anishinaabek and was raised in Thunder Bay, Ontario. Her program of research is driven by Indigenous concepts of decolonization through physical activity, health, and well-being.

DEVI MUCINA is an Assistant Professor in Indigenous Governance at the University of Victoria. As an Ubuntu African, Devi's scholarship is guided by a decolonizing intersectionality framework, which centres Indigenous international collaborative partnerships through dialogue about Indigenous decolonizing research. Devi is also the author of a forthcoming book. Ubuntu Relational Love: Decolonizing Indigenous Black Masculinities and Fathering (University of Manitoba press).

NO'EAU PERALTO (Kanaka 'Ōiwi) was born and raised in Waiākea Uka, Hilo, Hawai'i, and is a proud descendant of kūpuna from Koholālele, Hāmākua, Hawai'i. He is currently a PhD. candidate in Indigenous Politics at UH Mānoa. His dissertation explores the continuity of mo'olelo and mālama 'āina praxis in Hāmākua Hikina through the resurgence work of Hui Mālama i ke Ala 'Ūlili, a grassroots organization of which he is a founding member and the current president.

MAYA L. KAWAILANAOKEAWAIKI SAFFERY was raised in Kailua, Koʻolaupoko, Oʻahu and is an ongoing student of the language and culture of her ancestors. With a Bachelor's degree in Hawaiian Language and a Master's of Education in Teaching degree both from the University of Hawaiʻi at Mānoa (UH Mānoa), she is the Curriculum Specialist for Kawaihuelani Center for Hawaiian Language at UH Mānoa. She is also a PhD candidate in Education whose research is focused on how Hawaiian educators might begin the process of reclaiming and reframing our own theories and pedagogies of ʻāina education so that we can once again regain control of our Native educational practices and reassert our educational sovereignty.

MICK SCOW is from the Kwakwakaʼwakw and Snuneymuxw First Nations, representing the Scow and Good families, respectively. He is currently a Ph.D candidate in Indigenous Governance at the University of Victoria. His work focuses on decolonizing masculinities, with an emphasis on revitalizing Indigenous fatherhood and family-based resurgence. He currently lives on unceded, illegally occupied Lekwungen and W̱SÁNEĆ territories with his partner and their three children.

NOENOE K. SILVA (Kanaka Hawaiʻi), of Kailua, Oʻahu, serves as Professor of Hawaiian and Indigenous Politics and Hawaiian language at the University of Hawaiʻi at Mānoa. She is the author of The Power of the Steel-tipped Pen: Reconstructing Native Hawaiian Intellectual History and Aloha Betrayed: Native Hawaiian Resistance to American Colonialism, recognized as one of the ten most influential books in the first decade of the 21st century by the Native American and Indigenous Studies Association.

GINA STARBLANKET (Cree/Saulteaux) grew up in Regina and is a member of the Star Blanket Cree Nation in Treaty 4 territory. She lives and works in Treaty 1 territory as an Assistant Professor in Native Studies and Women's Studies with the University of Manitoba. Gina received her PhD from the Indigenous Governance program at the University of Victoria in 2017.

LISA STRELEIN is Executive Director of Research and Education at the Australian Institute of Aboriginal and Torres Strait Islander Studies. Lisa's research and publications have focused on the relationship between Indigenous peoples and the state, and the role of the courts in defining Indigenous peoples' rights. Dr Strelein has made a significant contribution to academic debate on native title in Australia, including her book: Compromised Jurisprudence: Native Title Cases since Mabo. Lisa maintains strong networks within the Indigenous peoples across Australia, conducting research projects in partnership with, or in response to, the needs of Indigenous organisations and regularly provides advice to government departments. She has degrees in Commerce and Law and a PhD from the Australian National University (ANU). Lisa is an Honorary Professor at the ANU and an visiting Professor at the University of Victoria, British Columbia.

JANA-RAE YERXA is Anishinaabe and her home community is Couchiching, First Nation which is located within Treaty #3 territory. Jana-Rae holds a Master of Social Work degree from Lakehead University and a Master of Arts degree, in Indigenous Governance, from the University of Victoria. Currently, Jana-Rae resides in Thunder Bay, Ontario and is the Coordinator for the Aboriginal Community Advocacy Program at Confederation College where she also teaches.

CPSIA information can be obtained
at www.ICGtesting.com
Printed in the USA
LVHW111604101219
640062LV00005B/869/P